PLAYS

THIRD SERIES

BY

JOHN GALSWORTHY

PLAYS

THIRD SERIES

THE FUGITIVE
THE PIGEON
THE MOB

BY

JOHN GALSWORTHY

NEW YORK
CHARLES SCRIBNER'S SONS
1915

𝕿𝖔
DOLORES AND FRANK LUCAS

THE FUGITIVE
A PLAY IN FOUR ACTS

PERSONS OF THE PLAY

GEORGE DEDMOND, *a civilian*
CLARE, *his wife*
GENERAL SIR CHARLES DEDMOND, K.C.B., *his father.*
LADY DEDMOND, *his mother*
REGINALD HUNTINGDON, *Clare's brother*
EDWARD FULLARTON ⎫ *her friends*
DOROTHY FULLARTON ⎭
PAYNTER, *a manservant*
BURNEY, *a maid*
TWISDEN, *a solicitor*
HAYWOOD, *a tobacconist*
MALISE, *a writer*
MRS. MILER, *his caretaker*
THE PORTER *at his lodgings*
A BOY *messenger*
ARNAUD, *a waiter at " The Gascony "*
MR. VARLEY, *manager of " The Gascony "*
TWO LADIES WITH LARGE HATS, A LADY AND GENTLEMAN, A
    LANGUID LORD, HIS COMPANION, A YOUNG MAN, A BLOND
    GENTLEMAN, A DARK GENTLEMAN.

ACT   I. *George Dedmond's Flat. Evening.*
ACT II. *The rooms of Malise. Morning.*
ACT III. SCENE I. *The rooms of Malise. Late afternoon.*
          SCENE II. *The rooms of Malise. Early After-*
              noon.
ACT IV. *A small supper room at " The Gascony."*

  Between Acts I and II three nights elapse.
  Between Acts II and Act III, Scene I, three months.
  Between Act III, Scene I, and Act III, Scene II, three
    months.
  Between Act III, Scene II, and Act IV six months.

CAST OF THE FIRST PRODUCTION

ROYAL COURT THEATRE, SEPTEMBER 16, 1913

George Dedmond	Mr. Claude King
Clare	Miss Irene Rooke
General Sir Charles Dedmond, K.C.B.	Mr. Nigel Playfair
Lady Dedmond	Miss Alma Murray
Reginald Huntingdon	Mr. Hylton Allen
Edward Fullarton	Mr. Leslie Rea
Mrs. Fullarton	Miss Estelle Winwood
Paynter	Mr. Frank Macrae
Burney	Miss Doris Bateman
Twisden	Mr. J. H. Roberts
Haywood	Mr. Charles Groves
Malise	Mr. Milton Rosmer
Mrs. Miler	Mrs. A. B. Tapping
Porter	Mr. Eric Barber
A Messenger Boy	

CHARACTERS IN ACT FOUR

A Young Man	Mr. Vincent Clive
Arnaud	Mr. Clarence Derwent
Mr. Varley	Mr. Charles Groves
A Languid Lord	Mr. J. H. Roberts
His Companion	Miss More-Dunphie
A Blond Gentleman	Mr. Leslie Rea
Two Ladies with large hats	Misses Bateman and Newcombe

ACT I

The SCENE is the pretty drawing-room of a flat. There are two doors, one open into the hall, the other shut and curtained. Through a large bay window, the curtains of which are not yet drawn, the towers of Westminster can be seen darkening in a summer sunset; a grand piano stands across one corner. The man-servant PAYNTER, clean-shaven and discreet, is arranging two tables for Bridge.

BURNEY, the maid, a girl with one of those flowery Botticellian faces only met with in England, comes in through the curtained door, which she leaves open, disclosing the glimpse of a white wall. PAYNTER looks up at her; she shakes her head, with an expression of concern.

PAYNTER. Where's she gone?

BURNEY. Just walks about, I fancy.

PAYNTER. She and the Governor don't hit it! One of these days she'll flit—you'll see. I like her—she's a lady; but these throughbred 'uns—it's their skin and their mouths. They'll go till they drop if they like the job, and if they don't, it's nothing but jib—jib—jib. How was it down there before she married him?

BURNEY. Oh! Quiet, of course.

1

PAYNTER. Country homes—I know 'em. What's her father, the old Rector, like?

BURNEY. Oh! very steady old man. The mother dead long before I took the place.

PAYNTER. Not a penny, I suppose?

BURNEY. [*Shaking her head*] No; and seven of them.

PAYNTER. [*At sound of the hall door*] The Governor!

> BURNEY *withdraws through the curtained door.*
>
> GEORGE DEDMOND *enters from the hall. He is in evening dress, opera hat, and overcoat; his face is broad, comely, glossily shaved, but with neat moustaches. His eyes, clear, small, and blue-grey, have little speculation. His hair is well brushed.*

GEORGE. [*Handing* PAYNTER *his coat and hat*] Look here, Paynter! When I send up from the Club for my dress things, always put in a black waistcoat as well.

PAYNTER. I asked the mistress, sir.

GEORGE. In future—see?

PAYNTER. Yes, sir. [*Signing towards the window*] Shall I leave the sunset, sir?

> But GEORGE *has crossed to the curtained door; he opens it and says:* "Clare!" *Receiving no answer, he goes in.* PAYNTER *switches up the electric light. His face, turned towards the curtained door, is apprehensive.*

GEORGE. [*Re-entering*] Where's Mrs. Dedmond?

PAYNTER. I hardly know, sir.

GEORGE. Dined in?

PAYNTER. She had a mere nothing at seven, sir.

GEORGE. Has she gone out, since?

PAYNTER. Yes, sir—that is, yes. The—er—mistress was not dressed at all. A little matter of fresh air, I think, sir.

GEORGE. What time did my mother say they'd be here for Bridge?

PAYNTER. Sir Charles and Lady Dedmond were coming at half-past nine; and Captain Huntingdon, too—Mr. and Mrs. Fullarton might be a bit late, sir.

GEORGE. It's that now. Your mistress said nothing?

PAYNTER. Not to me, sir.

GEORGE. Send Burney.

PAYNTER. Very good, sir.   [*He withdraws.*

> GEORGE *stares gloomily at the card tables.* BURNEY *comes in from the hall.*

GEORGE. Did your mistress say anything before she went out?

BURNEY. Yes, sir.

GEORGE. Well?

BURNEY. I don't think she meant it, sir.

GEORGE. I don't want to know what you don't think, I want the fact.

BURNEY. Yes, sir. The mistress said: "I hope it'll be a pleasant evening, Burney!"

GEORGE. Oh!—Thanks.

BURNEY. I've put out the mistress's things, sir.

GEORGE. Ah!

BURNEY. Thank you, sir.   [*She withdraws.*

GEORGE. Damn!

> *He again goes to the curtained door, and passes through.* PAYNTER, *coming in from the hall, announces:* "General Sir Charles and Lady Dedmond." SIR CHARLES *is an upright, well-groomed, grey-moustached, red-faced man of sixty-seven, with a keen eye for molehills, and none at all for mountains.* LADY DEDMOND *has a firm, thin face, full of capability and decision, not without kindliness; and faintly weathered, as if she had faced many situations in many parts of the world. She is fifty-five.*
>
> PAYNTER *withdraws.*

SIR CHARLES. Hullo! Where are they? H'm!

> *As he speaks,* GEORGE *re-enters.*

LADY DEDMOND. [*Kissing her son*] Well, George. Where's Clare?

GEORGE. Afraid she's late.

LADY DEDMOND. Are we early?

GEORGE. As a matter of fact, she's not in.

LADY DEDMOND. Oh?

SIR CHARLES. H'm! Not—not had a rumpus?

GEORGE. Not particularly. [*With the first real sign of feeling*] What I can't stand is being made a fool of before other people. Ordinary friction one can put up with. But that——

SIR CHARLES. Gone out on purpose? What!

LADY DEDMOND. What was the trouble?

GEORGE. I told her this morning you were coming in

to Bridge. Appears she'd asked that fellow Malise, for music.

LADY DEDMOND. Without letting you know?

GEORGE. I believe she did tell me.

LADY DEDMOND. But surely——

GEORGE. I don't want to discuss it. There's never anything in particular. We're all anyhow, as you know.

LADY DEDMOND. I see. [*She looks shrewdly at her son*] My dear, I should be rather careful about him, I think.

SIR CHARLES. Who's that?

LADY DEDMOND. That Mr. Malise.

SIR CHARLES. Oh! That chap!

GEORGE. Clare isn't that sort.

LADY DEDMOND. I know. But she catches up notions very easily. I think it's a great pity you ever came across him.

SIR CHARLES. Where did you pick him up?

GEORGE. Italy—this Spring—some place or other where they couldn't speak English.

SIR CHARLES. Um! That's the worst of travellin'.

LADY DEDMOND. I think you ought to have dropped him. These literary people— [*Quietly*] From exchanging ideas to something else, isn't very far, George.

SIR CHARLES. We'll make him play Bridge. Do him good, if he's that sort of fellow.

LADY DEDMOND. Is anyone else coming?

GEORGE. Reggie Huntingdon, and the Fullartons.

LADY DEDMOND. [*Softly*] You know, my dear boy,

I've been meaning to speak to you for a long time. It *is* such a pity you and Clare— What is it?

GEORGE. God knows! I try, and I believe she does.

SIR CHARLES. It's distressin' for us, you know, my dear fellow—distressin'.

LADY DEDMOND. I know it's been going on for a long time.

GEORGE. Oh! leave it alone, mother.

LADY DEDMOND. But, George, I'm afraid this man has brought it to a point—put ideas into her head.

GEORGE. You can't dislike him more than I do. But there's nothing one can object to.

LADY DEDMOND. Could Reggie Huntingdon do anything, now he's home? Brothers sometimes——

GEORGE. I can't bear my affairs being messed about with.

LADY DEDMOND. Well! it would be better for you and Clare to be supposed to be out together, than for her to be out alone. Go quietly into the dining-room and wait for her.

SIR CHARLES. Good! Leave your mother to make up something. She'll do it!

[*A bell sounds.*

LADY DEDMOND. That may be he. Quick!

GEORGE *goes out into the hall, leaving the door open in his haste.* LADY DEDMOND, *following, calls* "Paynter!" PAYNTER *enters.*

LADY DEDMOND. Don't say anything about your master and mistress being out. I'll explain.

PAYNTER. The master, my lady?

LADY DEDMOND. Yes, I know. But you needn't say so. Do you understand?

PAYNTER. [*In polite dudgeon*] Just so, my lady.

                                   [*He goes out.*

SIR CHARLES. By Jove! That fellow smells a rat!

LADY DEDMOND. Be careful, Charles!

SIR CHARLES. I should think so.

LADY DEDMOND. I shall simply say they're dining out, and that we're not to wait Bridge for them.

SIR CHARLES. [*Listening*] He's having a palaver with that man of George's.

    PAYNTER, *reappearing, announces:* "Captain Huntingdon." SIR CHARLES *and* LADY DEDMOND *turn to him with relief.*

LADY DEDMOND. Ah! It's you, Reginald!

HUNTINGDON. [*A tall, fair soldier, of thirty*] How d'you do? How are you, sir? What's the matter with their man?

SIR CHARLES. What!

HUNTINGDON. I was going into the dining-room to get rid of my cigar; and he said: "Not in there, sir. The master's there, but my instructions are to the effect that he's not."

SIR CHARLES. I knew that fellow——

LADY DEDMOND. The fact is, Reginald, Clare's out, and George is waiting for her. It's so important people shouldn't——

HUNTINGDON. Rather!

    They draw together, as people do, discussing the misfortunes of members of their families.

LADY DEDMOND. It's getting serious, Reginald. I don't know what's to become of them. You don't think the Rector—you don't think your father would speak to Clare?

HUNTINGDON. Afraid the Governor's hardly well enough. He takes anything of that sort to heart so —especially Clare.

SIR CHARLES. Can't you put in a word yourself?

HUNTINGDON. Don't know where the mischief lies.

SIR CHARLES. I'm sure George doesn't gallop her on the road. Very steady-goin' fellow, old George.

HUNTINGDON. Oh, yes; George is all right, sir.

LADY DEDMOND. They ought to have had children.

HUNTINGDON. Expect they're pretty glad now they haven't. I really don't know what to say, ma'am.

SIR CHARLES. Saving your presence, you know, Reginald, I've often noticed parsons' daughters grow up queer. Get too much morality and rice puddin'.

LADY DEDMOND. [*With a clear look*] Charles!

SIR CHARLES. What was she like when you were kids?

HUNTINGDON. Oh, all right. Could be rather a little devil, of course, when her monkey was up.

SIR CHARLES. I'm fond of her. Nothing she wants that she hasn't got, is there?

HUNTINGDON. Never heard her say so.

SIR CHARLES. [*Dimly*] I don't know whether old George is a bit too matter of fact for her. H'm?

[*A short silence.*

LADY DEDMOND. There's a Mr. Malise coming here to-night. I forget if you know him.

HUNTINGDON. Yes. Rather a thorough-bred mongrel.

LADY DEDMOND. He's literary. [*With hesitation*] You —you don't think he—puts—er—ideas into her head?

HUNTINGDON. I asked Greyman, the novelist, about him; seems he's a bit of an Ishmaelite, even among those fellows. Can't see Clare——

LADY DEDMOND. No. Only, the great thing is that she shouldn't be encouraged. Listen!—It *is* her—coming in. I can hear their voices. Gone to her room. What a blessing that man isn't here yet! [*The door bell rings*] Tt! There he is, I expect.

SIR CHARLES. What are we goin' to say?

HUNTINGDON. Say they're dining out, and we're not to wait Bridge for them.

SIR CHARLES. Good!

> *The door is opened, and* PAYNTER *announces* "Mr. Kenneth Malise." MALISE *enters. He is a tall man, about thirty-five, with a strongly-marked, dark, irregular, ironic face, and eyes which seem to have needles in their pupils. His thick hair is rather untidy, and his dress clothes not too new.*

LADY DEDMOND. How do you do? My son and daughter-in-law are so very sorry. They'll be here directly.

> [MALISE *bows with a queer, curly smile.*

SIR CHARLES. [*Shaking hands*] How d'you do, sir?

HUNTINGDON. We've met, I think.

He gives MALISE *that peculiar smiling stare, which seems to warn the person bowed to of the sort of person he is.* MALISE's *eyes sparkle.*

LADY DEDMOND. Clare will be so grieved. One of those invitations——

MALISE. On the spur of the moment.

SIR CHARLES. You play Bridge, sir?

MALISE. Afraid not!

SIR CHARLES. Don't mean that? Then we shall have to wait for 'em.

LADY DEDMOND. I forget, Mr. Malise—you write, don't you?

MALISE. Such is my weakness.

LADY DEDMOND. Delightful profession.

SIR CHARLES. Doesn't tie you! What!

MALISE. Only by the head.

SIR CHARLES. I'm always thinkin' of writin' my experiences.

MALISE. Indeed!

[*There is the sound of a door banged.*

SIR CHARLES. [*Hastily*] You smoke, Mr. Malise?

MALISE. Too much.

SIR CHARLES. Ah! Must smoke when you think a lot.

MALISE. Or think when you smoke a lot.

SIR CHARLES. [*Genially*] Don't know that I find that.

LADY DEDMOND. [*With her clear look at him*] Charles!

The door is opened. CLARE DEDMOND *in a*

cream-coloured evening frock comes in from the hall, followed by GEORGE. *She is rather pale, of middle height, with a beautiful figure, wavy brown hair, full, smiling lips, and large grey mesmeric eyes, one of those women all vibration, iced over with a trained stoicism of voice and manner.*

LADY DEDMOND. Well, my dear!

SIR CHARLES. Ah! George. Good dinner?

GEORGE. [*Giving his hand to* MALISE] How are you? Clare! Mr. Malise!

CLARE. [*Smiling—in a clear voice with the faintest possible lisp*] Yes, we met on the door-mat. [*Pause.*

SIR CHARLES. Deuce you did! [*An awkward pause.*

LADY DEDMOND. [*Acidly*] Mr. Malise doesn't play Bridge, it appears. Afraid we shall be rather in the way of music.

SIR CHARLES. What! Aren't we goin' to get a game?

[PAYNTER *has entered with a tray.*

GEORGE. Paynter! Take that table into the dining-room.

PAYNTER. [*Putting down the tray on a table behind the door*] Yes, sir.

MALISE. Let me give you a hand.

PAYNTER *and* MALISE *carry one of the Bridge tables out,* GEORGE *making a half-hearted attempt to relieve* MALISE.

SIR CHARLES. Very fine sunset!

Quite softly CLARE *begins to laugh. All look at her first with surprise, then with offence, then almost with horror.* GEORGE *is about to go up to her, but* HUNTINGDON *heads him off.*

HUNTINGDON. Bring the tray along, old man.

GEORGE *takes up the tray, stops to look at* CLARE, *then allows* HUNTINGDON *to shepherd him out.*

LADY DEDMOND. [*Without looking at* CLARE] Well, if we're going to play, Charles?   [*She jerks his sleeve.*

SIR CHARLES. What?   [*He marches out.*

LADY DEDMOND. [*Meeting* MALISE *in the doorway*] Now you will be able to have your music.

[*She follows the* GENERAL *out.*

[CLARE *stands perfectly still, with her eyes closed.*

MALISE. Delicious!

CLARE. [*In her level, clipped voice*] Perfectly beastly of me! I'm so sorry. I simply can't help running amok to-night.

MALISE. Never apologize for being fey. It's much too rare.

CLARE. On the door-mat! And they'd whitewashed me so beautifully! Poor dears! I wonder if I ought——

[*She looks towards the door.*

MALISE. Don't spoil it!

CLARE. I'd been walking up and down the Embankment for about three hours. One does get desperate sometimes.

MALISE. Thank God for that!

CLARE. Only makes it worse afterwards. It seems so frightful to them, too.

MALISE. [*Softly and suddenly, but with a difficulty*

in finding the right words] Blessed be the respectable! May they dream of—me! And blessed be all men of the world! May they perish of a surfeit of—good form!

CLARE. I like that. Oh, won't there be a row! [*With a faint movement of her shoulders*] And the usual reconciliation.

MALISE. Mrs. Dedmond, there's a whole world outside yours. Why don't you spread your wings?

CLARE. My dear father's a saint, and he's getting old and frail; and I've got a sister engaged; and three little sisters to whom I'm supposed to set a good example. Then, I've no money, and I can't do anything for a living, except serve in a shop. I shouldn't be free, either; so what's the good? Besides, I oughtn't to have married if I wasn't going to be happy. You see, I'm not a bit misunderstood or ill-treated. It's only——

MALISE. Prison. Break out!

CLARE. [*Turning to the window*] Did you see the sunset? That white cloud trying to fly up?

[*She holds up her bare arms, with a motion of flight.*

MALISE. [*Admiring her*] Ah-h-h! [*Then, as she drops her arms suddenly*] Play me something.

CLARE. [*Going to the piano*] I'm awfully grateful to you. *You* don't make me feel just an attractive female. I wanted somebody like that. [*Letting her hands rest on the notes*] All the same, I'm *glad* not to be ugly.

MALISE. Thank God for beauty!

PAYNTER. [*Opening the door*] Mr. and Mrs. Fullarton.

MALISE. Who are *they?*

CLARE. [*Rising*] She's my chief pal.   He was in the Navy.

> *She goes forward.* MRS. FULLARTON *is a rather tall woman, with dark hair and a quick eye. He, one of those clean-shaven naval men of good presence who have retired from the sea, but not from their susceptibility.*

MRS. FULLARTON. [*Kissing* CLARE, *and taking in both* MALISE *and her husband's look at* CLARE] We've only come for a minute.

CLARE. They're playing Bridge in the dining-room. Mr. Malise doesn't play.   Mr. Malise—Mrs. Fullarton, Mr. Fullarton.

> [*They greet.*

FULLARTON. Most awfully jolly dress, Mrs. Dedmond.

MRS. FULLARTON. Yes, lovely, Clare. [FULLARTON *abases eyes which mechanically readjust themselves*] We can't stay for Bridge, my dear; I just wanted to see you a minute, that's all. [*Seeing* HUNTINGDON *coming in she speaks in a low voice to her husband*] Edward, I want to speak to Clare. How d'you do, Captain Huntingdon?

MALISE. I'll say good-night.

> *He shakes hands with* CLARE, *bows to* MRS. FULLARTON, *and makes his way out.* HUNTINGDON *and* FULLARTON *foregather in the doorway.*

MRS. FULLARTON. How *are* things, Clare? [CLARE *just moves her shoulders*] Have you done what I suggested? Your room?

CLARE. No.

MRS. FULLARTON. Why not?

CLARE. I don't want to torture him. If I strike— I'll go clean. I expect I *shall* strike.

MRS. FULLARTON. My dear! You'll have the whole world against you.

CLARE. Even you won't back me, Dolly?

MRS. FULLARTON. Of course I'll back you, all that's possible, but I can't invent things.

CLARE. You wouldn't let me come to you for a bit, till I could find my feet?

> MRS. FULLARTON, *taken aback, cannot refrain from her glance at* FULLARTON *automatically gazing at* CLARE *while he talks with* HUNTINGDON.

MRS. FULLARTON. Of course—the only thing is that——

CLARE. [*With a faint smile*] It's all right, Dolly. I'm not coming.

MRS. FULLARTON. Oh! don't do anything desperate, Clare—you are so desperate sometimes. You ought to make terms—not tracks.

CLARE. Haggle? [*She shakes her head*] What have I got to make terms with? What he still wants is just what I hate giving.

MRS. FULLARTON. But, Clare——

CLARE. No, Dolly; even you don't understand. All day and every day—just as far apart as we can be— and still— Jolly, isn't it? If you've got a soul at all.

MRS. FULLARTON. It's awful, really.

CLARE. I suppose there are lots of women who feel as I do, and go on with it; only, you see, I happen to have something in me that—comes to an end. Can't endure beyond a certain time, ever.

> *She has taken a flower from her dress, and suddenly tears it to bits. It is the only sign of emotion she has given.*

MRS. FULLARTON. [*Watching*] Look here, my child; this won't do. You must get a rest. Can't Reggie take you with him to India for a bit?

CLARE. [*Shaking her head*] Reggie lives on his pay.

MRS. FULLARTON. [*With one of her quick looks*] That was Mr. Malise, then?

FULLARTON. [*Coming towards them*] I say, Mrs. Dedmond, you wouldn't sing me that little song you sang the other night, [*He hums*] "If I might be the falling bee and kiss thee all the day"? Remember?

MRS. FULLARTON. "The falling *dew*," Edward. We simply must go, Clare. Good-night. [*She kisses her.*

FULLARTON. [*Taking half-cover between his wife and* CLARE] It suits you down to the ground—that dress.

CLARE. Good-night.

> HUNTINGDON *sees them out. Left alone* CLARE *clenches her hands, moves swiftly across to the window, and stands looking out.*

HUNTINGDON. [*Returning*] Look here, Clare!

CLARE. Well, Reggie?

HUNTINGDON. This is working up for a mess, old girl. You can't do this kind of thing with impunity. No man'll put up with it. If you've got anything against George, better tell me. [CLARE *shakes her head*] You ought to know I should stick by you. What is it? Come?

CLARE. Get married, and find out after a year that she's the wrong person; so wrong that you can't exchange a single real thought; that your blood runs cold when she kisses you—then you'll know.

HUNTINGDON. My dear old girl, I don't want to be a brute; but it's a bit difficult to believe in that, except in novels.

CLARE. Yes, incredible, when you haven't tried.

HUNTINGDON. I mean, you—you chose him yourself. No one forced you to marry him.

CLARE. It does seem monstrous, doesn't it?

HUNTINGDON. My dear child, do give us a reason.

CLARE. Look! [*She points out at the night and the darkening towers*] If George saw that for the first time he'd just say, "Ah, Westminster! Clock Tower! Can you see the time by it?" As if one cared where or what it was—beautiful like that! Apply that to every —every—everything.

HUNTINGDON. [*Staring*] George may be a bit prosaic. But, my dear old girl, if that's all——

CLARE. It's not all—it's nothing. I can't explain, Reggie—it's not reason, at all; it's—it's like being underground in a damp cell; it's like knowing you'll never get out.   Nothing coming—never anything coming again—never anything.

HUNTINGDON. [*Moved and puzzled*] My dear old thing; you mustn't get into fantods like this. If it's like that, don't think about it.

CLARE. When every day and every night!— Oh! I know it's my fault for having married him, but that doesn't help.

HUNTINGDON. Look here! It's not as if George wasn't quite a decent chap. And it's no use blinking things; you *are* absolutely dependent on him. At home they've got every bit as much as they can do to keep going.

CLARE. I know.

HUNTINGDON. And you've got to think of the girls. Any trouble would be very beastly for them. And the poor old Governor would feel it awfully.

CLARE. If I didn't know all that, Reggie, I should have gone home long ago.

HUNTINGDON. Well, what's to be done? If my pay would run to it—but it simply won't.

CLARE. Thanks, old boy, of course not.

HUNTINGDON. Can't you try to see George's side of it a bit?

CLARE. I *do*. Oh! don't let's talk about it.

HUNTINGDON. Well, my child, there's just one thing —you won't go sailing near the wind, will you? I mean, there are fellows always on the lookout.

CLARE. "That chap, Malise, you'd better avoid him!" Why?

HUNTINGDON. Well! I don't know him. He may be all right, but he's not our sort. And you're too pretty to go on the tack of the New Woman and that kind of thing—haven't been brought up to it.

CLARE. British home-made summer goods, light and attractive—don't wear long. [*At the sound of voices in the hall*] They seem to be going, Reggie.

   [HUNTINGDON *looks at her, vexed, unhappy.*

HUNTINGDON. Don't head for trouble, old girl. Take a pull. Bless you! Good-night.

   CLARE *kisses him, and when he has gone turns away from the door, holding herself in, refusing to give rein to some outburst of emotion. Suddenly she sits down at the untouched Bridge table, leaning her bare elbows on it and her chin on her hands, quite calm.* GEORGE *is coming in.* PAYNTER *follows him.*

CLARE. Nothing more wanted, thank you, Paynter. You can go home, and the maids can go to bed.

PAYNTER. We are much obliged, ma'am.

CLARE. I ran over a dog, and had to get it seen to.

PAYNTER. Naturally, ma'am!

CLARE. Good-night.

PAYNTER. I couldn't get you a little anything, ma'am?

CLARE. No, thank you.

PAYNTER. No, ma'am. Good-night, ma'am.

   [*He withdraws.*

GEORGE. You needn't have gone out of your way to tell a lie that wouldn't deceive a guinea-pig. [*Going up to her*] Pleased with yourself to-night? [CLARE *shakes her head*] Before that fellow Malise; as if our own people weren't enough!

CLARE. Is it worth while to rag me? I know I've behaved badly, but I couldn't help it, really!

GEORGE. Couldn't help behaving like a shop-girl? My God! You were brought up as well as I was.

CLARE. Alas!

GEORGE. To let everybody see that we don't get on —there's only one word for it—Disgusting!

CLARE. I know.

GEORGE. Then why do you do it? I've always kept *my* end up. Why in heaven's name do you behave in this crazy way?

CLARE. I'm sorry.

GEORGE. [*With intense feeling*] You like making a fool of me!

CLARE. No— Really! Only—I must break out sometimes.

GEORGE. There are things one does not do.

CLARE. I came in because I was sorry.

GEORGE. And at once began to do it again! It seems to me you delight in rows.

CLARE. You'd miss your—reconciliations.

GEORGE. For God's sake, Clare, drop cynicism!

CLARE. And truth?

GEORGE. You are my wife, I suppose.

CLARE. And they twain shall be one—spirit.

GEORGE. Don't talk wild nonsense!

[*There is silence.*

CLARE. [*Softly*] I *don't* give satisfaction. Please give me notice!

GEORGE. Pish!

CLARE. Five years, and four of them like this! I'm sure we've served our time. Don't you really think we might get on better together—if I went away?

GEORGE. I've told you I won't stand a separation for no real reason, and have your name bandied about all over London. I have some primitive sense of honour.

CLARE. You mean *your* name, don't you?

GEORGE. Look here. Did that fellow Malise put all this into your head?

CLARE. No; my own evil nature.

GEORGE. I wish the deuce we'd never met him. Comes of picking up people you know nothing of. I distrust him—and his looks—and his infernal satiric way. He can't even dress decently. He's not—good form.

CLARE. [*With a touch of rapture*] Ah-h!

GEORGE. Why do you let him come? What d'you find interesting in him?

CLARE. A mind.

GEORGE. Deuced funny one! To have a mind—as you call it—it's not necessary to talk about Art and Literature.

CLARE. We don't.

GEORGE. Then what do you talk about—your minds? [CLARE *looks at him*] Will you answer a straight question? Is he falling in love with you?

CLARE. You had better ask him.

GEORGE. I tell you plainly, as a man of the world, I don't believe in the guide, philosopher and friend business.

CLARE. Thank you.

A silence. CLARE suddenly clasps her hands behind her head.

CLARE. Let me go! You'd be much happier with any other woman.

GEORGE. Clare!

CLARE. I believe—I'm sure I could earn my living. Quite serious.

GEORGE. Are you mad?

CLARE. It has been done.

GEORGE. It will never be done by you—understand that!

CLARE. It really is time we parted. I'd go clean out of your life. I don't want your support unless I'm giving you something for your money.

GEORGE. Once for all, I don't mean to allow you to make fools of us both.

CLARE. But if we are already! Look at us. We go on, and on. We're a spectacle!

GEORGE. That's not my opinion; nor the opinion of anyone, so long as you behave yourself.

CLARE. That is—behave as you think right.

GEORGE. Clare, you're pretty riling.

CLARE. I don't want to be horrid. But I am in earnest this time.

GEORGE. So am I.

> [CLARE *turns to the curtained door.*

GEORGE. Look here! I'm sorry.　God knows I don't want to be a brute.　I know you're not happy.

CLARE. And you—are you happy?

GEORGE. I don't say I am.　But why can't we be?

CLARE. I see no reason, except that you are you, and I am I.

GEORGE. We can try.

CLARE. I *have*—haven't you?

GEORGE. We used——

CLARE. I wonder!

GEORGE. You know we did.

CLARE. Too long ago—if ever.

GEORGE [*Coming closer*] I—still——

CLARE. [*Making a barrier of her hand*] You know that's only cupboard love.

GEORGE. We've got to face the facts.

CLARE. I thought I was.

GEORGE. The facts are that we're married—for better or worse, and certain things are expected of us.　It's suicide for you, and folly for me, in my position, to ignore that.　You have all you can reasonably want; and I don't—don't wish for any change.　If you could bring anything against me—if I drank, or knocked about town, or expected too much of you. I'm not unreasonable in any way, that I can see.

CLARE. Well, I think we've talked enough.

> [*She again moves towards the curtained door.*

GEORGE. Look here, Clare; you don't mean you're

expecting me to put up with the position of a man who's neither married nor unmarried? That's simple purgatory. You ought to know.

CLARE. Yes. I haven't yet, have I?

GEORGE. Don't go like that! Do you suppose we're the only couple who've found things aren't what they thought, and have to put up with each other and make the best of it.

CLARE. Not by thousands.

GEORGE. Well, why do you imagine they do it?

CLARE. I don't know.

GEORGE. From a common sense of decency.

CLARE. Very!

GEORGE. By Jove! You can be the most maddening thing in all the world! [*Taking up a pack of cards, he lets them fall with a long slithering flutter*] After behaving as you have this evening, you might try to make some amends, I should think.

> CLARE *moves her head from side to side, as if in sight of something she could not avoid. He puts his hand on her arm.*

CLARE. No, no—no!

GEORGE. [*Dropping his hand*] Can't you make it up?

CLARE. I don't feel very Christian.

> *She opens the door, passes through, and closes it behind her.* GEORGE *steps quickly towards it, stops, and turns back into the room. He goes to the window and stands looking out ; shuts it with a bang, and again contemplates the door. Moving forward, he rests his hand on the de-*

*serted card table, clutching its edge, and mut-
tering.   Then he crosses to the door into the hall
and switches off the light.   He opens the door to
go out, then stands again irresolute in the darkness and heaves a heavy sigh.   Suddenly he mut-
ters: "No!"   Crosses resolutely back to the
curtained door, and opens it.   In the gleam of
light* CLARE *is standing, unhooking a necklet.
He goes in, shutting the door behind him with a
thud.*

CURTAIN.

ACT II

*The Scene is a large, whitewashed, disordered room,
whose outer door opens on to a corridor and stairway.
Doors on either side lead to other rooms. On the
walls are unframed reproductions of fine pictures,
secured with tintacks. An old wine-coloured armchair of low and comfortable appearance, near the
centre of the room, is surrounded by a litter of manu-
scripts, books, ink, pens and newspapers, as though
some one had already been up to his neck in labour,
though by a grandfather's clock it is only eleven.
On a smallish table close by, are sheets of paper,
cigarette ends, and two claret bottles. There are
many books on shelves, and on the floor, an over-
flowing pile, whereon rests a soft hat, and a black
knobby stick. MALISE sits in his armchair, garbed
in trousers, dressing-gown, and slippers, unshaved
and uncollared, writing. He pauses, smiles, lights
a cigarette, and tries the rhythm of the last sentence,
holding up a sheet of quarto MS.*

MALISE. "Not a word, not a whisper of Liberty from
all those excellent frock-coated gentlemen—not a sign,
not a grimace. Only the monumental silence of their
profound deference before triumphant Tyranny."

*While he speaks, a substantial woman, a little
over middle-age, in old dark clothes and a black*

27

straw hat, enters from the corridor. She goes
to a cupboard, brings out from it an apron and
a Bissell broom. Her movements are slow and
imperturbable, as if she had much time before
her. Her face is broad and dark, with Chinese
eyebrows.

MALISE. Wait, Mrs. Miler!

MRS. MILER. I'm gettin' be'ind'and, sir.

> *She comes and stands before him.* MALISE
> *writes.*

MRS. MILER. There's a man 'angin' about below.

> MALISE *looks up; seeing that she has roused his*
> *attention, she stops. But as soon as he is about*
> *to write again, goes on.*

MRS. MILER. I see him first yesterday afternoon.
I'd just been out to get meself a pennyworth o' soda, an'
as I come in I passed 'im on the second floor, lookin' at
me with an air of suspicion. I thought to meself at the
time, I thought: You're a 'andy sort of 'ang-dog man.

MALISE. Well?

MRS. MILER. Well—peekin' down through the bal-
usters, I see 'im lookin' at a photograft. That's a
funny place, I thinks, to look at pictures—it's so dark
there, ye 'ave to use yer eyesight. So I giv' a scrape
with me 'eel [*She illustrates*] an' he pops it in his
pocket, and puts up 'is 'and to knock at number three.
I goes down an' I says: "You know there's no one lives
there, don't yer?" "Ah!" 'e says with an air of inner-
cence, "I wants the name of Smithers." "Oh!" I says,
"try round the corner, number ten." "Ah!" 'e says,

tactful, "much obliged." "Yes," I says, "you'll find 'im in at this time o' day. Good evenin'!" And I thinks to meself [*She closes one eye*] Rats! There's a good many corners hereabouts.

MALISE. [*With detached appreciation*] Very good, Mrs. Miler.

MRS. MILER. So this mornin', there e' was again on the first floor with 'is 'and raised, pretendin' to knock at number two. "Oh! you're still lookin' for 'im?" I says, lettin' him see I was 'is grandmother. "Ah!" 'e says, affable, "you misdirected me; it's here I've got my business." "That's lucky," I says, "cos nobody lives there neither. Good mornin'!" And I come straight up. If you want to see 'im at work you've only to go downstairs, 'e'll be on the ground floor by now, pretendin' to knock at number one. Wonderful resource!

MALISE. What's he like, this gentleman?

MRS. MILER. Just like the men you see on the front page o' the daily papers. Nasty, smooth-lookin' feller, with one o' them billycock hats you can't abide.

MALISE. Isn't he a dun?

MRS. MILER. *They* don't be'ave like that; *you* ought to know, sir. He's after no good. [*Then, after a little pause*] Ain't he to be put a stop to? If I took me time I could get 'im, innercent-like, with a jug o' water.

[MALISE, *smiling, shakes his head.*

MALISE. You can get on now; I'm going to shave.

He looks at the clock, and passes out into the inner room. MRS. MILER *gazes round her, pins up her skirt, sits down in the armchair, takes off her hat and puts it on the table, and slowly rolls up her sleeves; then with her hands on her knees she rests. There is a soft knock on the door. She gets up leisurely and moves flat-footed towards it. The door being opened* CLARE *is revealed.*

CLARE. Is Mr. Malise in?

MRS. MILER. Yes. But 'e's dressin'.

CLARE. Oh.

MRS. MILER. Won't take 'im long. What name?

CLARE. Would you say—a lady.

MRS. MILER. It's against the rules. But if you'll sit down a moment I'll see what I can do. [*She brings forward a chair and rubs it with her apron. Then goes to the door of the inner room and speaks through it*] A lady to see you. [*Returning she removes some cigarette ends*] This is my hour. I shan't make much dust. [*Noting* CLARE'S *eyebrows raised at the débris round the armchair*] I'm particular about not disturbin' things.

CLARE. I'm sure you are.

MRS. MILER. He likes 'is 'abits regular.

Making a perfunctory pass with the Bissell broom, she runs it to the cupboard, comes back to the table, takes up a bottle and holds it to the light; finding it empty, she turns it upside down and drops it into the wastepaper basket; then, holding up the other bottle, and finding it not empty, she corks it and drops it into the fold of her skirt.

MRS. MILER. He takes his claret fresh-opened—not like these 'ere bawgwars.

CLARE. [*Rising*] I think I'll come back later.

MRS. MILER. Mr. Malise is not in my confidence. We keep each other to ourselves.   Perhaps you'd like to read the paper; he has it fresh every mornin'—the *Westminister.*

> *She plucks that journal from out of the armchair and hands it to* CLARE, *who sits down again unhappily to brood.* MRS. MILER *makes a pass or two with a very dirty duster, then stands still.   No longer hearing sounds,* CLARE *looks up.*

MRS. MILER. I wouldn't interrupt yer with my workin,' but 'e likes things clean. [*At a sound from the inner room*] That's 'im; 'e's cut 'isself!   I'll just take 'im the tobaccer!

> *She lifts a green paper screw of tobacco from the débris round the armchair and taps on the door. It opens.* CLARE *moves restlessly across the room.*

MRS. MILER. [*Speaking into the room*] The tobaccer. The lady's waitin'.

> CLARE *has stopped before a reproduction of Titian's picture "Sacred and Profane Love."* MRS. MILER *stands regarding her with a Chinese smile.* MALISE *enters, a thread of tobacco still hanging to his cheek.*

MALISE. [*Taking* MRS. MILER'S *hat off the table and handing it to her*] Do the other room.

> [*Enigmatically she goes.*

MALISE. Jolly of you to come.   Can I do anything?

CLARE. I want advice—badly.

MALISE. What! Spreading your wings?

CLARE. Yes.

MALISE. Ah! Proud to have given you *that* advice. When?

CLARE. The morning after you gave it me . . .

MALISE. Well?

CLARE. I went down to my people. I knew it would hurt my Dad frightfully, but somehow I thought I could make him see. No good. He was awfully sweet, only—he couldn't.

MALISE. [*Softly*] We English love liberty in those who don't belong to us. Yes.

CLARE. It was horrible. There were the children— and my old nurse. I could never live at home now. They'd think I was——. Impossible—utterly! I'd made up my mind to go back to my owner— And then —he came down himself. I couldn't stand it. To be hauled back and begin all over again; I simply couldn't. I watched for a chance; and ran to the station, and came up to an hotel.

MALISE. Bravo!

CLARE. I don't know—no pluck this morning! You see, I've got to earn my living—no money; only a few things I can sell. All yesterday I was walking about, looking at the women. How does anyone ever get a chance?

MALISE. Sooner than you should hurt his dignity by working, your husband would pension you off.

CLARE. If I don't go back to him I couldn't take it.

MALISE. Good!

CLARE. I've thought of nursing, but it's a long train-ing, and I do so hate watching pain. The fact is, I'm pretty hopeless; can't even do art work. I came to ask you about the stage.

MALISE. Have you ever acted? [CLARE *shakes her head*] You mightn't think so, but I've heard there's a prejudice in favour of training. There's Chorus—I don't recommend it. How about your brother?

CLARE. My brother's got nothing to spare, and he wants to get married; and he's going back to India in September. The only friend I should care to bother is Mrs. Fullarton, and she's—got a husband.

MALISE. I remember the gentleman.

CLARE. Besides, I should be besieged day and night to go back. I must lie doggo somehow.

MALISE. It makes my blood boil to think of women like you. God help all ladies without money.

CLARE. I expect I shall have to go back.

MALISE. No, no! We shall find something. Keep your soul alive at all costs. What! let him hang on to you till you're nothing but—emptiness and ache, till you lose even the power to ache. Sit in his drawing-room, pay calls, play Bridge, go out with him to din-ners, return to—duty; and feel less and less, and be less and less, and so grow old and—die!

[*The bell rings.*

MALISE. [*Looking at the door in doubt*] By the way—he'd no means of tracing you?

[*She shakes her head.*
[*The bell rings again.*

MALISE. Was there a man on the stairs as you came up?

CLARE. Yes. Why?

MALISE. He's begun to haunt them, I'm told.

CLARE. Oh! But that would mean they thought I —oh! no!

MALISE. Confidence in *me* is not excessive.

CLARE. Spying!

MALISE. Will you go in there for a minute? Or shall we let them ring—or—what? It may not be anything, of course.

CLARE. I'm not going to hide.

[*The bell rings a third time.*

MALISE. [*Opening the door of the inner room*] Mrs. Miler, just see who it is; and then go, for the present.

MRS. MILER *comes out with her hat on, passes enigmatically to the door, and opens it. A man's voice says:* "Mr. Malise? Would you give him these cards?"

MRS. MILER. [*Re-entering*] The cards.

MALISE. Mr. Robert Twisden. Sir Charles and Lady Dedmond. [*He looks at* CLARE.

CLARE. [*Her face scornful and unmoved*] Let them come.

MALISE. [*To* MRS. MILER] Show them in!

TWISDEN *enters—a clean-shaved, shrewd-looking man, with a fighting underlip, followed by* SIR CHARLES *and* LADY DEDMOND. MRS. MILER *goes. There are no greetings.*

TWISDEN. Mr. Malise? How do you do, Mrs. Dedmond? Had the pleasure of meeting you at your wedding. [CLARE *inclines her head*] I am Mr. George Dedmond's solicitor, sir. I wonder if you would be so very kind as to let us have a few words with Mrs. Dedmond alone?

> *At a nod from* CLARE, MALISE *passes into the inner room, and shuts the door. A silence.*

SIR CHARLES. [*Suddenly*] What!

LADY DEDMOND. Mr. Twisden, will you——?

TWISDEN. [*Uneasy*] Mrs. Dedmond——I must apologize, but you—you hardly gave us an alternative, did you? [*He pauses for an answer, and, not getting one, goes on*] Your disappearance has given your husband great anxiety. Really, my dear madam, you must forgive us for this—attempt to get into communication.

CLARE. Why did you spy *here?*

SIR CHARLES. No, no! Nobody's spied on you. What!

TWISDEN. I'm afraid the answer is that we appear to have been justified. [*At the expression on* CLARE's *face he goes on hastily*] Now, Mrs. Dedmond, I'm a lawyer and I know that appearances are misleading. Don't think I'm unfriendly; I wish you well. [CLARE *raises her eyes. Moved by that look, which is exactly as if she had said: "I have no friends," he hurries on*] What we want to say to you is this: Don't let this split go on! Don't commit yourself to what you'll bitterly regret. Just tell us what's the matter. I'm sure it can be put straight.

CLARE. I have nothing against my husband—it was quite unreasonable to leave him.

TWISDEN. Come, that's good.

CLARE. Unfortunately, there's something stronger than reason.

TWISDEN. I don't know it, Mrs. Dedmond.

CLARE. No?

TWISDEN. [*Disconcerted*] Are you—you oughtn't to take a step without advice, in your position.

CLARE. Nor with it?

TWISDEN. [*Approaching her*] Come, now; isn't there anything you feel you'd like to say—that might help to put matters straight?

CLARE. I don't think so, thank you.

LADY DEDMOND. You must see, Clare, that——

TWISDEN. In your position, Mrs. Dedmond—a beautiful young woman without money. I'm quite blunt. This is a hard world. Should be awfully sorry if anything goes wrong.

CLARE. And if I go back?

TWISDEN. Of two evils, if it be so—choose the least!

CLARE. I am twenty-six; he is thirty-two. We can't reasonably expect to die for fifty years.

LADY DEDMOND. That's morbid, Clare.

TWISDEN. What's open to you if you don't go back? Come, what's your position? Neither fish, flesh, nor fowl; fair game for everybody. Believe me, Mrs. Dedmond, for a pretty woman to strike, as it appears you're doing, simply because the spirit of her marriage has taken flight, is madness. You must know that no

one pays attention to anything but facts. If now—
excuse me—you—you had a lover, [*His eyes travel
round the room and again rest on her*] you would, at all
events, have some ground under your feet, some sort
of protection, but [*He pauses*] as you have not—you've
none.

CLARE. Except what I make myself.

SIR CHARLES. Good God!

TWISDEN. Yes! Mrs. Dedmond! There's the bed-
rock difficulty. As you haven't money, you should
never have been pretty. You're up against the world,
and you'll get no mercy from it. We lawyers see too
much of that. I'm putting it brutally, as a man of the
world.

CLARE. Thank you. Do you think you quite grasp
the alternative?

TWISDEN. [*Taken aback*] But, my dear young lady,
there are two sides to every contract. After all, your
husband's fulfilled his.

CLARE. So have I up till now. I shan't ask anything from him—nothing—do you understand?

LADY DEDMOND. But, my dear, you must live.

TWISDEN. Have you ever done any sort of work?

CLARE. Not yet.

TWISDEN. Any conception of the competition nowadays?

CLARE. I can try.

[TWISDEN, *looking at her, shrugs his shoulders.*

CLARE. [*Her composure a little broken by that look*]
It's real to me—this—you see!

SIR CHARLES. But, my dear girl, what the devil's to become of George?

CLARE. He can do what he likes—it's nothing to me.

TWISDEN. Mrs. Dedmond, I say without hesitation you've no notion of what you're faced with, brought up to a sheltered life as you've been. Do realize that you stand at the parting of the ways, and one leads into the wilderness.

CLARE. Which?

TWISDEN. [*Glancing at the door through which* MALISE *has gone*] Of course, if you want to play at wild asses there are plenty who will help you.

SIR CHARLES. By Gad! Yes!

CLARE. I only want to breathe.

TWISDEN. Mrs. Dedmond, go back! You can now. It will be too late soon. There are lots of wolves about.

[*Again he looks at the door.*

CLARE. But not where you think. You say I need advice. I came here for it.

TWISDEN. [*With a curiously expressive shrug*] In that case I don't know that I can usefully stay.

[*He goes to the outer door.*

CLARE. Please don't have me followed when I leave here. Please!

LADY DEDMOND. George is outside, Clare.

CLARE. I don't wish to see him. By what right have you come here? [*She goes to the door through which* MALISE *has passed, opens it, and says*] Please come in, Mr. Malise.

MALISE *enters.*

TWISDEN. I am sorry. [*Glancing at* MALISE, *he inclines his head*] I am sorry. Good morning. [*He goes.*

LADY DEDMOND. Mr. Malise, I'm sure, will see——

CLARE. Mr. Malise will stay here, please, in his own room. [MALISE *bows.*

SIR CHARLES. My dear girl, 'pon my soul, you know, I can't grasp your line of thought at all!

CLARE. No?

LADY DEDMOND. George is most willing to take up things just as they were before you left.

CLARE. Ah!

LADY DEDMOND. Quite frankly—what is it you want?

CLARE. To be left alone. Quite frankly, he made a mistake to have me spied on.

LADY DEDMOND. But, my good girl, if you'd let us know where you were, like a reasonable being. You can't possibly be left to yourself without money or position of any kind. Heaven knows what you'd be driven to! [*She looks at* MALISE.

MALISE. [*Softly*] Delicious!

SIR CHARLES. You will be good enough to repeat that out loud, sir.

LADY DEDMOND. Charles! Clare, you must know this is all a fit of spleen; your duty and your interest —marriage is sacred, Clare.

CLARE. Marriage! *My* marriage has become the— the reconciliation—of two animals—one of them unwilling. That's all the sanctity there is about it.

SIR CHARLES. What!

LADY DEDMOND. You ought to be horribly ashamed.

CLARE. Of the fact—I am.

LADY DEDMOND. [*Darting a glance at* MALISE] If we are to talk this out, it must be in private.

MALISE. [*To* CLARE] Do you wish me to go?

CLARE. No.

LADY DEDMOND. [*At* MALISE] I should have thought ordinary decent feeling—— Good heavens, girl! Can't you see that you're being played with?

CLARE. If you insinuate anything against Mr. Malise, you lie.

LADY DEDMOND. If you *will* do these things—come to a man's rooms——

CLARE. I came to Mr. Malise because he's the only person I know with imagination enough to see what my position is; I came to him a quarter of an hour ago, for the first time, for definite advice, and you instantly suspect him. That is disgusting.

LADY DEDMOND. [*Frigidly*] Is this the natural place for me to find my son's wife?

CLARE. His woman.

LADY DEDMOND. Will you listen to Reginald?

CLARE. I have.

LADY DEDMOND. Haven't you any religious sense at all, Clare?

CLARE. None, if it's religion to live as we do.

LADY DEDMOND. It's terrible—this state of mind! It's really terrible!

> CLARE *breaks into the soft laugh of the other evening. As if galvanized by the sound,* SIR

CHARLES *comes to life out of the transfixed bewilderment with which he has been listening.*

SIR CHARLES. For God's sake don't laugh like that!

[CLARE *stops.*

LADY DEDMOND. [*With real feeling*] For the sake of the simple right, Clare!

CLARE. Right? Whatever else is right—*our* life is not. [*She puts her hand on her heart*] I swear before God that I've tried and tried. I swear before God, that if I believed we could ever again love each other only a little tiny bit, I'd go back. I swear before God that I don't want to hurt anybody.

LADY DEDMOND. But you are hurting everybody. Do—do be reasonable!

CLARE. [*Losing control*] Can't you see that I'm fighting for all my life to come—not to be buried alive —not to be slowly smothered. Look at me! I'm not wax—I'm flesh and blood. And you want to prison me for ever—body and soul.

[*They stare at her.*

SIR CHARLES. [*Suddenly*] By Jove! I don't know, I don't know! What!

LADY DEDMOND. [*To* MALISE] If you have any decency left, sir, you will allow my son, at all events, to speak to his wife alone. [*Beckoning to her husband*] We'll wait below.

SIR CHARLES. I—I want to speak. [*To* CLARE] My dear, if you feel like this, I can only say as a—as a gentleman——

LADY DEDMOND. Charles!

SIR CHARLES. Let me alone! I can only say that —damme, I don't know that I can say anything!

> *He looks at her very grieved, then turns and marches out, followed by* LADY DEDMOND, *whose voice is heard without, answered by his:* "What!" *In the doorway, as they pass,* GEORGE *is standing; he comes in.*

GEORGE. [*Going up to* CLARE, *who has recovered all her self-control*] Will you come outside and speak to me?

CLARE. No.

> GEORGE *glances at* MALISE, *who is leaning against the wall with folded arms.*

GEORGE. [*In a low voice*] Clare!

CLARE. Well!

GEORGE. You try me pretty high, don't you, forcing me to come here, and speak before this fellow? Most men would think the worst, finding you like this.

CLARE. You need not have come—or thought at all.

GEORGE. Did you imagine I was going to let you vanish without an effort——

CLARE. To save me?

GEORGE. For God's sake be just! I've come here to say certain things. If you force me to say them before him—on your head be it! Will you appoint somewhere else?

CLARE. No.

GEORGE. Why not?

CLARE. I know all those "certain things." "You must come back. It is your duty. You have no money. Your friends won't help you. You can't earn your living.   You are making a scandal."   You might even say for the moment: "Your room shall be respected."

GEORGE. Well, it's true and you've no answer.

CLARE. Oh! [*Suddenly*] Our life's a lie.   It's stupid; it's disgusting.   I'm tired of it!   Please leave me alone!

GEORGE. You rather miss the point, I'm afraid.   I didn't come here to tell you what you know perfectly well when you're sane.   I came here to say this: Anyone in her senses could see the game your friend here is playing.   It wouldn't take a baby in.   If you think that a gentleman like that [*His stare travels round the dishevelled room till it rests on* MALISE] champions a pretty woman for nothing, you make a fairly bad mistake.

CLARE. Take care.

> *But* MALISE, *after one convulsive movement of his hands, has again become rigid.*

GEORGE. I don't pretend to be subtle or that kind of thing; but I have ordinary common sense.   I don't attempt to be superior to plain facts——

CLARE. [*Under her breath*] Facts!

GEORGE. Oh! for goodness' sake drop that hifalutin' tone.   It doesn't suit you.   Look here!   If you like to go abroad with one of your young sisters until the autumn, I'll let the flat and go to the Club.

CLARE. Put the fire out with a penny hose. [*Slowly*] I am not coming back to you, George.   The farce is over.

GEORGE. [*Taken aback for a moment by the finality of her tone, suddenly fronts* MALISE] Then there *is* something between you and this fellow.

MALISE. [*Dangerously, but without moving*] I beg your pardon!

CLARE. There—is—nothing.

GEORGE [*Looking from one to the other*] At all events, I won't—I won't see a woman who once— [CLARE *makes a sudden effacing movement with her hands*] I won't see her go to certain ruin without lifting a finger.

CLARE. That is noble.

GEORGE. [*With intensity*] I don't know that you deserve anything of me. But on my honour, as a gentleman, I came here this morning for your sake, to warn you of what you're doing. [*He turns suddenly on* MALISE] And I tell this precious friend of yours plainly what I think of him, and that I'm not going to play into his hands.

> MALISE, *without stirring from the wall, looks at* CLARE, *and his lips move.*

CLARE. [*Shakes her head at him—then to* GEORGE] Will you go, please?

GEORGE. I will go when you do.

MALISE. A man of the world should know better than that.

GEORGE. Are you coming?

MALISE. That is inconceivable.

GEORGE. I'm not speaking to you, sir.

MALISE. You are right. Your words and mine will never kiss each other.

GEORGE. Will you come? [CLARE *shakes her head.*

GEORGE. [*With fury*] D'you mean to stay in this pigsty with that rhapsodical swine?

MALISE. [*Transformed*] By God, if you don't go, I'll kill you.

GEORGE. [*As suddenly calm*] That remains to be seen.

MALISE. [*With most deadly quietness*] Yes, I will *kill* you.

> *He goes stealthily along the wall, takes up from where it lies on the pile of books the great black knobby stick, and stealthily approaches* GEORGE, *his face quite fiendish.*

CLARE. [*With a swift movement, grasping the stick*] Please.

> MALISE *resigns the stick, and the two men, perfectly still, glare at each other.* CLARE, *letting the stick fall, puts her foot on it. Then slowly she takes off her hat and lays it on the table.*

CLARE. *Now* will you go!   [*There is silence.*

GEORGE. [*Staring at her hat*] You mad little fool! Understand this; if you've not returned home by three o'clock I'll divorce you, and you may roll in the gutter with this high-souled friend of yours. And mind this, you sir—I won't spare you—by God! Your pocket shall suffer. That's the only thing that touches fellows like you.

> *Turning, he goes out, and slams the door.* CLARE *and* MALISE *remain face to face. Her lips have begun to quiver.*

CLARE. Horrible!

> *She turns away, shuddering, and sits down on the edge of the armchair, covering her eyes with the backs of her hands.* MALISE *picks up the stick, and fingers it lovingly. Then putting it down, he moves so that he can see her face. She is sitting quite still, staring straight before her.*

MALISE. Nothing could be better.

CLARE. I don't know what to do! I don't know what to do!

MALISE. Thank the stars for your good fortune.

CLARE. He means to have revenge on you! And it's all my fault.

MALISE. Let him. Let him go for his divorce. Get rid of him. Have done with him—somehow.

> *She gets up and stands with face averted. Then swiftly turning to him.*

CLARE. If I must bring you harm—let me pay you back! I can't bear it otherwise! Make some use of me, if you don't mind!

MALISE. My God!

> [*She puts up her face to be kissed, shutting her eyes.*

MALISE. You poor——

> *He clasps and kisses her, then, drawing back, looks in her face. She has not moved, her eyes are still closed; but she is shivering; her lips are tightly pressed together; her hands twitching.*

MALISE. [*Very quietly*] No, no! This is not the house of a "gentleman."

CLARE. [*Letting her head fall, and almost in a whisper*] I'm sorry.

MALISE. I understand.

CLARE. I don't feel.   And without—I can't, can't.

MALISE. [*Bitterly*] Quite right.   You've had enough of *that*.

> *There is a long silence.   Without looking at him she takes up her hat, and puts it on.*

MALISE. Not going?   [CLARE *nods.*

MALISE. You don't trust me?

CLARE. I *do!*   But I can't take when I'm not giving.

MALISE. I beg—I beg you!   What does it matter? Use me!   Get free somehow.

CLARE. Mr. Malise, I know what I ought to be to you, if I let you in for all this.   I know what you want—or will want.   Of course—why not?

MALISE. I give you my solemn word——

CLARE. No! if I can't be *that* to you—it's not real. And I *can't*.   It isn't to be manufactured, is it?

MALISE. It is not.

CLARE. To make use of you in such a way!   No.

> [*She moves towards the door.*

MALISE. *Where* are you going?

> CLARE *does not answer.   She is breathing rapidly. There is a change in her, a sort of excitement beneath her calmness.*

MALISE. Not back to *him?* [CLARE *shakes her head*] Thank God!   But where?   To your people again?

CLARE. No.

MALISE. Nothing—desperate?

CLARE. Oh! no.

MALISE. Then what—tell me—come!

CLARE. I don't know. Women manage somehow.

MALISE. But *you*—poor dainty thing!

CLARE. It's all right! Don't be unhappy! Please!

MALISE. [*Seizing her arm*] D'you imagine they'll let you off, out there—you with your face? Come, trust me—trust me! You must!

CLARE. [*Holding out her hand*] Good-bye!

MALISE. [*Not taking that hand*] This great damned world, and—you! Listen! [*The sound of the traffic far down below is audible in the stillness*] Into *that!* alone— helpless—without money. The men who work with you; the men you make friends of—d'you think they'll let you be? The men in the streets, staring at you, stopping you—pudgy, bull-necked brutes; devils with hard eyes; senile swine; and the "chivalrous" men, like me, who don't mean you harm, but can't help seeing you're made for love! Or suppose you *don't* take covert but struggle on in the open. Society! The respectable! The pious! Even those who love you! Will they let you be? Hue and cry! The hunt was joined the moment you broke away! It will never let up! Covert to covert—till they've run you down, and you're back in the cart, and God pity you!

CLARE. Well, I'll die running!

MALISE. No, no! Let me shelter you! Let me!

CLARE. [*Shaking her head and smiling*] I'm going to seek my fortune. Wish me luck!

MALISE. I *can't* let you go.

CLARE. You *must*.

> *He looks into her face; then, realizing that she means it, suddenly bends down to her fingers, and puts his lips to them.*

MALISE. Good luck, then! Good luck!

> *He releases her hand. Just touching his bent head with her other hand,* CLARE *turns and goes.* MALISE *remains with bowed head, listening to the sound of her receding footsteps. They die away. He raises himself, and strikes out into the air with his clenched fist.*

CURTAIN.

ACT III

MALISE'S *sitting-room. An afternoon, three months later. On the table are an open bottle of claret, his hat, and some tea-things. Down in the hearth is a kettle on a lighted spirit-stand. Near the door stands* HAYWOOD, *a short, round-faced man, with a tobacco-coloured moustache;* MALISE, *by the table, is contemplating a piece of blue paper.*

HAYWOOD. Sorry to press an old customer, sir, but a year and an 'alf without any return on your money——

MALISE. Your tobacco is too good, Mr. Haywood. I wish I could see my way to smoking another.

HAYWOOD. Well, sir—that's a funny remedy.

> *With a knock on the half-opened door, a* BOY *appears.*

MALISE. Yes. What is it?

BOY. Your copy for "The Watchfire," please, sir.

MALISE. [*Motioning him out*] Yes. Wait!

> *The* BOY *withdraws.* MALISE *goes up to the pile of books, turns them over, and takes up some volumes.*

MALISE. This is a very fine unexpurgated translation of Boccaccio's "Decameron," Mr. Haywood—illustrated. I should say you would get more than the amount of your bill for them.

51

HAYWOOD. [*Shaking his head*] Them books worth three pound seven!

MALISE. It's scarce, and highly improper. Will you take them in discharge?

HAYWOOD. [*Torn between emotions*] Well, I 'ardly know what to say— No, sir, I don't think I'd like to 'ave to do with that.

MALISE. You could read them first, you know?

HAYWOOD. [*Dubiously*] I've got my wife at 'ome.

MALISE. You could both read them.

HAYWOOD. [*Brought to his bearings*] No, sir, I couldn't.

MALISE. Very well; I'll sell them myself, and you shall have the result.

HAYWOOD. Well, thank you, sir. I'm sure I didn't want to trouble you.

MALISE. Not at all, Mr. Haywood. It's for me to apologize.

HAYWOOD. So long as I give satisfaction.

MALISE. [*Holding the door for him*] Certainly. Good evening.

HAYWOOD. Good evenin', sir; no offence, I hope.

MALISE. On the contrary.

> *Doubtfully* HAYWOOD *goes. And* MALISE *stands scratching his head; then slipping the bill into one of the volumes to remind him, he replaces them at the top of the pile. The* BOY *again advances into the doorway.*

MALISE. Yes, now for you.

> *He goes to the table and takes some sheets of MS.*

*from an old portfolio.   But the door is again
timidly pushed open, and* HAYWOOD *reappears.*

MALISE. Yes, Mr. Haywood?

HAYWOOD. About that little matter, sir. If—if it's
any convenience to you—I've—thought of a place
where I could——

MALISE. Read them? You'll enjoy them thor-
oughly.

HAYWOOD. No, sir, no! Where I can dispose of
them.

MALISE. [*Holding out the volumes*] It might be as
well. [HAYWOOD *takes the books gingerly*] I congratu-
late you, Mr. Haywood; it's a classic.

HAYWOOD. Oh, indeed—yes, sir. In the event of
there being any——

MALISE. Anything over? Carry it to my credit.
Your bill—— [*He hands over the blue paper*] Send me
the receipt.   Good evening!

> HAYWOOD, *nonplussed, and trying to hide the
> books in an evening paper, fumbles out :* "Good
> evenin', sir!" *and departs.* MALISE *again
> takes up the sheets of MS. and cons a sentence
> over to himself, gazing blankly at the stolid*
> BOY.

MALISE. "Man of the world—good form your god!
Poor buttoned-up philosopher" [*the* BOY *shifts his feet*]
"inbred to the point of cretinism, and founded to the
bone on fear of ridicule [*the* BOY *breathes heavily*]—you
are the slave of facts!"

> [*There is a knock on the door.*

MALISE. Who is it?

> *The door is pushed open, and* REGINALD HUNT-
> INGDON *stands there.*

HUNTINGDON. I apologize, sir; can I come in a minute?

> [MALISE *bows with ironical hostility.*

HUNTINGDON. I don't know if you remember me—Clare Dedmond's brother.

MALISE. I remember you.

> [*He motions to the stolid* BOY *to go outside again.*

HUNTINGDON. I've come to you, sir, as a gentleman——

MALISE. Some mistake. There is one, I believe, on the first floor

HUNTINGDON. It's about my sister.

MALISE. D—n you! Don't you know that I've been shadowed these last three months? Ask your detectives for any information you want.

HUNTINGDON. We know that you haven't seen her, or even known where she is.

MALISE. Indeed! You've found that out? Brilliant!

HUNTINGDON. We know it from my sister.

MALISE. Oh! So you've tracked her down?

HUNTINGDON. Mrs. Fullarton came across her yesterday in one of those big shops—selling gloves.

MALISE. Mrs. Fullarton—the lady with the husband. Well! you've got her. Clap her back into prison.

HUNTINGDON. We have not got her. She left at once, and we don't know where she's gone.

MALISE. Bravo!

HUNTINGDON. [*Taking hold of his bit*] Look here, Mr. Malise, in a way I share your feeling, but I'm fond of my sister, and it's damnable to have to go back to India knowing she must be all adrift, without protection, going through God knows what! Mrs. Fullarton says she's looking awfully pale and down.

MALISE. [*Struggling between resentment and sympathy*] Why do you come to me?

HUNTINGDON. We thought——

MALISE. *Who?*

HUNTINGDON. My—my father and myself.

MALISE. Go on.

HUNTINGDON. We thought there was just a chance that, having lost that job, she might come to you again for advice. If she does, it would be really generous of you if you'd put my father in touch with her. He's getting old, and he feels this very much. [*He hands* MALISE *a card*] This is his address.

MALISE. [*Twisting the card*] Let there be no mistake, sir; I do nothing that will help give her back to her husband. She's out to save her soul alive, and I don't join the hue and cry that's after her. On the contrary —if I had the power. If your father wants to shelter her, that's another matter. But she'd her own ideas about that.

HUNTINGDON. Perhaps you don't realize how unfit my sister is for rough and tumble. She's not one of this new sort of woman. She's always been looked after, and had things done for her. Pluck she's got, but that's all, and she's bound to come to grief.

MALISE. Very likely—the first birds do. But if she drops half-way it's better than if she'd never flown. Your sister, sir, is trying the wings of her spirit, out of the old slave market. For women as for men, there's more than one kind of dishonour, Captain Huntingdon, and worse things than being dead, as you may know in your profession.

HUNTINGDON. Admitted—but——

MALISE. We each have our own views as to what they are. But they all come to—death of our spirits, for the sake of our carcases. Anything more?

HUNTINGDON. My leave's up. I sail to-morrow. If you do see my sister I trust you to give her my love and say I begged she would see my father.

MALISE. If I have the chance—yes.

> *He makes a gesture of salute, to which* HUNTING- *DON responds. Then the latter turns and goes out.*

MALISE. Poor fugitive! Where are you running now?

> *He stands at the window, through which the even- ing sunlight is powdering the room with smoky gold. The stolid* BOY *has again come in.* MA- LISE *stares at him, then goes back to the table, takes up the MS., and booms it at him; he re- ceives the charge, breathing hard.*

MALISE. "Man of the world—product of a material age; incapable of perceiving reality in motions of the spirit; having 'no use,' as you would say, for 'sentimental nonesnse'; accustomed to believe yourself the national spine—your position is unassailable.   You will remain the idol of the country—arbiter of law, parson in mufti, darling of the playwright and the novelist —God bless you!—while waters lap these shores."

He places the sheets of MS. in an envelope, and hands them to the BOY.

MALISE.   You're going straight back to "The Watch-fire"?

BOY.   [*Stolidly*] Yes, sir.

MALISE.   [*Staring at him*] You're a masterpiece. D'you know that?

BOY.   No, sir.

MALISE.   Get out, then.

He lifts the portfolio from the table, and takes it into the inner room.   The BOY, *putting his thumb stolidly to his nose, turns to go.   In the doorway he shies violently at the figure of* CLARE, *standing there in a dark-coloured dress, skids past her and goes.   CLARE comes into the gleam of sunlight, her white face alive with emotion or excitement.   She looks round her, smiles, sighs; goes swiftly to the door, closes it, and comes back to the table.   There she stands, fingering the papers on the table, smoothing* MA-LISE'S *hat—wistfully, eagerly, waiting.*

MALISE.   [*Returning*] You!

CLARE.   [*With a faint smile*] Not very glorious, is it? *He goes towards her, and checks himself, then slews the armchair round.*

MALISE. Come! Sit down, sit down! [CLARE, *heaving a long sigh, sinks down into the chair*] Tea's nearly ready.

> *He places a cushion for her, and prepares tea; she looks up at him softly, but as he finishes and turns to her, she drops that glance.*

CLARE. Do you think me an awful coward for coming? [*She has taken a little plain cigarette case from her dress*] Would you mind if I smoked?

> MALISE *shakes his head, then draws back from her again, as if afraid to be too close. And again, unseen, she looks at him.*

MALISE. So you've lost your job?

CLARE. How did you——?

MALISE. Your brother. You only just missed him. [CLARE *starts up*] They had an idea you'd come. He's sailing to-morrow—he wants you to see your father.

CLARE. Is father ill?

MALISE. Anxious about you.

CLARE. I've written to him every week. [*Excited*] They're still hunting me!

MALISE. [*Touching her shoulder gently*] It's all right —all right.

> *She sinks again into the chair, and again he withdraws. And once more she gives him that soft eager look, and once more averts it as he turns to her.*

CLARE. My nerves have gone funny lately. It's being always on one's guard, and stuffy air, and feeling

people look and talk about you, and dislike your being
there.

MALISE. Yes; that wants pluck.

CLARE. [*Shaking her head*] I curl up all the time.
The only thing I know for certain is, that I shall never
go back to him. The more I've hated what I've been
doing, the more sure I've been. I might come to anything—but not that.

MALISE. Had a very bad time?

CLARE. [*Nodding*] I'm spoilt. It's a curse to be a
lady when you have to earn your living. It's not really
been so hard, I suppose; I've been selling things, and
living about twice as well as most shop girls.

MALISE. Were they decent to you?

CLARE. Lots of the girls are really nice. But somehow they don't want me, can't help thinking I've got
airs or something; and in here [*She touches her breast*]
I don't want them!

MALISE. I know.

CLARE. Mrs. Fullarton and I used to belong to a
society for helping reduced gentlewomen to get work.
I know now what they want: enough money *not* to
work—that's all! [*Suddenly looking up at him*] Don't
think me worse than I am—please! It's working *under* people; it's *having* to do it, being driven. I *have*
tried, I've not been altogether a coward, really! But
every morning getting there the same time; every day
the same stale "dinner," as they call it; every evening
the same "Good evening, Miss Clare," "Good evening,
Miss Simpson," "Good evening, Miss Hart," "Good
evening, Miss Clare." And the same walk home, or

the same 'bus; and the same men that you mustn't look at, for fear they'll follow you. [*She rises*] Oh! and the feeling—always, always—that there's no sun, or life, or hope, or anything. It was just like being ill, the way I've wanted to ride and dance and get out into the country. [*Her excitement dies away into the old clipped composure, and she sits down again*] Don't think too badly of me—it really is pretty ghastly!

MALISE. [*Gruffly*] H'm! Why a shop?

CLARE. References. I didn't want to tell more lies than I could help; a married woman on strike can't tell the truth, you know. And I can't typewrite or do shorthand yet. And chorus—I thought—*you* wouldn't like.

MALISE. I? What have I——? [*He checks himself*] Have men been brutes?

CLARE. [*Stealing a look at him*] One followed me a lot. He caught hold of my arm one evening. I just took this out [*She draws out her hatpin and holds it like a dagger, her lip drawn back as the lips of a dog going to bite*] and said: "Will you leave me alone, please?" And he did. It was rather nice. And there was one quite decent little man in the shop—I was sorry for *him*—such a humble little man!

MALISE. Poor devil—it's hard not to wish for the moon.

At the tone of his voice CLARE *looks up at him; his face is turned away.*

CLARE. [*Softly*] How have *you* been? Working very hard?

MALISE. As hard as God will let me.

CLARE. [*Stealing another look*] Have you any type-writing I could do? I could learn, and I've still got a brooch I could sell. Which is the best kind?

MALISE. I had a catalogue of them somewhere.

> *He goes into the inner room. The moment he is gone,* CLARE *stands up, her hands pressed to her cheeks as if she felt them flaming. Then, with hands clasped, she stands waiting. He comes back with the old portfolio.*

MALISE. Can you typewrite where you are?

CLARE. I have to find a new room anyway. I'm changing—to be safe. [*She takes a luggage ticket from her glove*] I took my things to Charing Cross—only a bag and one trunk. [*Then, with that queer expression on her face which prefaces her desperations*] You don't want me now, I suppose.

MALISE. What?

CLARE. [*Hardly above a whisper*] Because—if you still wanted me—I do—now.

MALISE. [*Staring hard into her face that is quivering and smiling*] You mean it? You *do?* You care——?

CLARE. I've thought of you—so much! But only—if you're sure.

> *He clasps her and kisses her closed eyes; and so they stand for a moment, till the sound of a latchkey in the door sends them apart.*

MALISE. It's the housekeeper. Give me that ticket; I'll send for your things.

> *Obediently she gives him the ticket, smiles, and goes quietly into the inner room.* MRS. MILER

> *has entered ; her face, more Chinese than ever, shows no sign of having seen.*

MALISE. That lady will stay here, Mrs. Miler. Kindly go with this ticket to the cloak-room at Charing Cross station, and bring back her luggage in a cab. Have you money?

MRS. MILER. 'Arf a crown. [*She takes the ticket— then impassively*] In case you don't know—there's two o' them men about the stairs now.

> *The moment she is gone* MALISE *makes a gesture of maniacal fury. He steals on tiptoe to the outer door, and listens. Then, placing his hand on the knob, he turns it without noise, and wrenches back the door. Transfigured in the last sunlight streaming down the corridor are two men, close together, listening and consulting secretly. They start back.*

MALISE. [*With strange, almost noiseless ferocity*] You've run her to earth; your job's done. Kennel up, hounds! [*And in their faces he slams the door.*

CURTAIN.

SCENE II

SCENE II.—*The same, early on a winter afternoon, three months later. The room has now a certain daintiness. There are curtains over the doors, a couch under the window, all the books are arranged on shelves. In small vases, over the fireplace, are a few violets and chrysanthemums.* MALISE *sits huddled in his armchair drawn close to the fire, paper on knee, pen in hand. He looks rather grey and drawn, and round his chair is the usual litter. At the table, now nearer to the window,* CLARE *sits working a typewriter. She finishes a line, puts sheets of paper together, makes a note on a card— adds some figures, and marks the total.*

CLARE. Kenneth, when this is paid, I shall have made two pound seventeen in the three months, and saved you about three pounds. One hundred and seventeen shillings at tenpence a thousand is one hundred and forty thousand words at fourteen hundred words an hour. It's only just over an hour a day. *Can't* you get me more?

> MALISE *lifts the hand that holds his pen and lets it fall again.* CLARE *puts the cover on the typewriter, and straps it.*

CLARE. I'm quite packed. Shall I pack for you? [*He nods*] Can't we have more than three days at the sea? [*He shakes his head. Going up to him*] You *did* sleep last night.

MALISE. Yes, I slept.

CLARE. Bad head? [MALISE *nods*] By this time the day after to-morrow the case will be heard and done with. You're not worrying for me? Except for my poor old Dad, *I* don't care a bit.

> MALISE *heaves himself out of the chair, and begins pacing up and down.*

CLARE. Kenneth, do you understand why he doesn't claim damages, after what he said that day—here? [*Looking suddenly at him*] It *is* true that he doesn't?

MALISE. It is not.

CLARE. But you told me yourself——

MALISE. I lied.

CLARE. Why?

MALISE. [*Shrugging*] No use lying any longer—you'd know it to-morrow.

CLARE. How much am I valued at?

MALISE. Two thousand. [*Grimly*] He'll settle it on you. [*He laughs*] Masterly! By one stroke, destroys his enemy, avenges his "honour," and gilds his name with generosity!

CLARE. Will you *have* to pay?

MALISE. Stones yield no blood.

CLARE. Can't you borrow?

MALISE. I couldn't even get the costs.

CLARE. Will they make you bankrupt, then? [MALISE *nods*] But that doesn't mean that you won't have your *income*, does it? [MALISE *laughs*] What is your income, Kenneth? [*He is silent*] A hundred and fifty from "The Watchfire," I know. What else?

MALISE. Out of five books I have made the sum of forty pounds.

CLARE. What else? Tell me.

MALISE. Fifty to a hundred pounds a year. Leave me to gnaw my way out, child.

> CLARE *stands looking at him in distress, then goes quickly into the room behind her.* MALISE *takes up his paper and pen. The paper is quite blank.*

MALISE. [*Feeling his head*] Full of smoke.

> *He drops paper and pen, and crossing to the room on the left goes in.* CLARE *re-enters with a small leather box. She puts it down on her typing table as* MALISE *returns followed by* MRS. MILER, *wearing her hat, and carrying his overcoat.*

MRS. MILER. Put your coat on. It's a bitter wind.
> [*He puts on the coat.*

CLARE. Where are you going?

MALISE. To "The Watchfire."

> *The door closes behind him, and* MRS. MILER *goes up to* CLARE *holding out a little blue bottle with a red label, nearly full.*

MRS. MILER. You know he's takin' this [*She makes a little motion towards her mouth*] to make 'im sleep?

CLARE. [*Reading the label*] Where was it?

MRS. MILER. In the bathroom chest o' drawers, where 'e keeps 'is odds and ends. I was lookin' for 'is garters.

CLARE. Give it to me!

MRS. MILER. He took it once before. He must get his sleep.

CLARE. Give it to me!

> MRS. MILER *resigns it*, CLARE *takes the cork out, smells, then tastes it from her finger.* MRS. MILER, *twisting her apron in her hands, speaks.*

MRS. MILER. I've 'ad it on my mind a long time to speak to yer. Your comin' 'ere's not done 'im a bit o' good.

CLARE. Don't!

MRS. MILER. I don't want to, but what with the worry o' this 'ere divorce suit, an' you bein' a lady an' 'im havin' to be so careful of yer, and tryin' to save, not smokin' all day like 'e used, an' not gettin' 'is two bottles of claret regular; an' losin' his sleep, an' takin' that stuff for it; and now this 'ere last business. I've seen 'im sometimes holdin' 'is 'ead as if it was comin' off. [*Seeing* CLARE *wince, she goes on with a sort of compassion in her Chinese face*] I can see yer fond of him; an' I've nothin' against yer—you don't trouble me a bit; but I've been with 'im eight years—we're used to each other, and I can't bear to see 'im not 'imself, really I can't.

> *She gives a sudden sniff. Then her emotion passes, leaving her as Chinese as ever.*

CLARE. This last business—what do you mean by that?

MRS. MILER. If 'e a'n't told yer, I don't know that I've any call to.

CLARE. Please.

Mrs. Miler. [*Her hands twisting very fast*] Well, it's to do with this 'ere "Watchfire." One of the men that sees to the writin' of it—'e's an old friend of Mr. Malise, 'e come 'ere this mornin' when you was out. I was doin' my work in there [*She points to the room on the right*] an' the door open, so I 'eard 'em. Now you've 'ung them curtains, you can't 'elp it.

Clare. Yes?

Mrs. Miler. It's about your divorce case. This 'ere "Watchfire," ye see, belongs to some fellers that won't 'ave their men gettin' into the papers. So this 'ere friend of Mr. Malise—very nice 'e spoke about it—"If it comes into Court," 'e says, "you'll 'ave to go," 'e says. "These beggars, these dogs, these logs," 'e says, "they'll 'oof you out," 'e says. An' I could tell by the sound of his voice, 'e meant it—proper upset 'e was. So that's that!

Clare. It's inhuman!

Mrs. Miler. That's what I thinks; but it don't 'elp, do it? "'Tain't the circulation," 'e says, "it's the principle," 'e says; and then 'e starts in swearin' horrible. 'E's a very nice man. And Mr. Malise, 'e says: "Well, that about does for me!" 'e says.

Clare. Thank you, Mrs. Miler—I'm glad to know.

Mrs. Miler. Yes; I don't know as I ought to 'ave told you. [*Desperately uncomfortable*] You see, I don't take notice of Mr. Malise, but I know 'im very well. 'E's a good-'earted gentleman, very funny, that'll do things to help others, and what's more, keep on doin' 'em, when they hurt 'im; very obstinate 'e is. Now, when you first come 'ere, three months ago, I says to meself: "He'll enjoy this 'ere for a bit, but she's too much of a lady for 'im." What 'e wants about 'im permanent is a woman that thinks an' talks about all them things he talks about. And sometimes I fancy 'e don't want nothin' permanent about 'im at all.

CLARE. Don't!

MRS. MILER. [*With another sudden sniff*] Gawd knows I don't want to upset ye. You're situated very 'ard; an' women's got no business to 'urt one another —that's what I thinks.

CLARE. Will you go out and do something for me? [MRS. MILER *nods.* CLARE *takes up the sheaf of papers and from the leather box a note and an emerald pendant*] Take this with the note to that address—it's quite close. He'll give you thirty pounds for it. Please pay these bills and bring me back the receipts, and what's over.

MRS. MILER. [*Taking the pendant and note*] It's a pretty thing.

CLARE. Yes. It was my mother's.

MRS. MILER. It's a pity to part with it; ain't you got another?

CLARE. Nothing more, Mrs. Miler, not even a wedding ring.

MRS. MILER. [*Without expression*] You make my 'eart ache sometimes.

> *She wraps pendant and note into her handkerchief and goes out to the door.*

MRS. MILER. [*From the door*] There's a lady and

gentleman out here. Mrs. Fuller—wants *you*, not Mr. Malise.

CLARE. Mrs. Fullarton? [MRS. MILER *nods*] Ask them to come in.

> MRS. MILER *opens the door wide, says* "Come in," *and goes.* MRS. FULLARTON *is accompanied not by* FULLARTON, *but by the lawyer,* TWISDEN. *They come in.*

MRS. FULLARTON. Clare! My dear! How are you after all this time?

CLARE. [*Her eyes fixed on* TWISDEN] Yes?

MRS. FULLARTON. [*Disconcerted by the strange greeting*] I brought Mr. Twisden to tell you something. May I stay?

CLARE. Yes. [*She points to the chair at the same table:* MRS. FULLARTON *sits down*] Now!

> [TWISDEN *comes forward.*

TWISDEN. As you're not defending this case, Mrs. Dedmond, there is nobody but yourself for me to apply to.

CLARE. Please tell me quickly, what you've come for.

TWISDEN. [*Bowing slightly*] I am instructed by Mr. Dedmond to say that if you will leave your present companion and undertake not to see him again, he will withdraw the suit and settle three hundred a year on you. [*At* CLARE's *movement of abhorrence*] Don't misunderstand me, please—it is not—it could hardly be, a request that you should go back. Mr. Dedmond is *not* prepared to receive you again. The proposal—forgive my saying so—remarkably Quixotic

—is made to save the scandal to his family and your own. It binds you to nothing but the abandonment of your present companion, with certain conditions of the same nature as to the future. In other words, it assures you a position—so long as you live quietly by yourself.

CLARE. I see. Will you please thank Mr. Dedmond, and say that I refuse?

MRS. FULLARTON. Clare, Clare! For God's sake don't be desperate.

[CLARE, *deathly still, just looks at her.*

TWISDEN. Mrs. Dedmond, I am bound to put the position to you in its naked brutality. You know there's a claim for damages?

CLARE. I have just learnt it.

TWISDEN. You realize what the result of this suit must be: You will be left dependent on an undischarged bankrupt. To put it another way, you'll be a stone round the neck of a drowning man.

CLARE. You are cowards.

MRS. FULLARTON. Clare, Clare! [*To* TWISDEN] She doesn't mean it; *please* be patient.

CLARE. I *do* mean it. You ruin him because of me. You get him down, and kick him to intimidate me.

MRS. FULLARTON. My dear girl! Mr. Twisden is not personally concerned. How can you?

CLARE. If I were dying, and it would save me, I wouldn't take a penny from my husband.

TWISDEN. Nothing could be more bitter than those

words. Do you really wish me to take them back to him?

CLARE. Yes.   [*She turns from them to the fire.*

MRS. FULLARTON. [*In a low voice to* TWISDEN] Please leave me alone with her, don't say anything to Mr. Dedmond yet.

TWISDEN. Mrs. Dedmond, I told you once that I wished you well. Though you have called me a coward, I still do that. For God's sake, think—before it's too late.

CLARE. [*Putting out her hand blindly*] I'm sorry I called you a coward. It's the whole thing, I meant.

TWISDEN. Never mind that. Think!

> *With the curious little movement of one who sees something he does not like to see, he goes.* CLARE *is leaning her forehead against the mantelshelf, seemingly unconscious that she is not alone.* MRS. FULLARTON *approaches quietly till she can see* CLARE'S *face.*

MRS. FULLARTON. My dear sweet thing, don't be cross with *me!* [CLARE *turns from her. It is all the time as if she were trying to get away from words and people to something going on within herself*] How can I help wanting to see you saved from all this ghastliness?

CLARE. Please don't, Dolly! Let me be!

MRS. FULLARTON. I must speak, Clare! I do think you're hard on George. It's generous of him to offer to withdraw the suit—considering. You do owe it to us to try and spare your father and your sisters and—and all of us who care for you.

CLARE. [*Facing her*] You say George is generous! If he wanted to be that he'd never have claimed those damages. It's revenge he wants—I heard him here. You think I've done him an injury. So I did—when I married him. I don't know what I shall come to, Dolly, but I shan't fall so low as to take money from him. That's as certain as that I shall die.

MRS. FULLARTON. Do you know, Clare, I think it's awful about you! You're too fine, and not fine enough, to put up with things; you're too sensitive to take help, and you're not strong enough to do without it. It's simply tragic. At any rate, you might go home to your people—

CLARE. After *this!*

MRS. FULLARTON. To us, then?

CLARE. "If I could be the falling bee, and kiss thee all the day!" No, Dolly! .

> MRS. FULLARTON *turns from her ashamed and baffled, but her quick eyes take in the room, trying to seize on some new point of attack.*

MRS. FULLARTON. You can't be—you aren't—happy, *here?*

CLARE. Aren't I?

MRS. FULLARTON. Oh! Clare! Save yourself—and all of us!

CLARE. [*Very still*] You see, I love him.

MRS. FULLARTON. You used to say you'd never love; did not want it—would never want it.

CLARE. Did I? How funny!

MRS. FULLARTON. Oh! my dear! Don't look like that, or you'll make me cry.

CLARE. One doesn't always know the future, does one? [*Desperately*] I love him! I love him!

MRS. FULLARTON. [*Suddenly*] If you love him, what will it be like for you, knowing you've ruined him?

CLARE. Go away! Go away!

MRS. FULLARTON. Love!—you said!

CLARE. [*Quivering at that stab—suddenly*] I must— I will keep him. He's all I've got.

MRS. FULLARTON. Can you—*can* you keep him?

CLARE. Go!

MRS. FULLARTON. I'm going. But, men are hard to keep, even when you've not been the ruin of them. You know whether the love this man gives you is really love. If not—God help you! [*She turns at the door, and says mournfully*] Good-bye, my child! If you can——

> *Then goes.* CLARE, *almost in a whisper, repeats the words:* "Love! you said!" *At the sound of a latchkey she runs as if to escape into the bed-room, but changes her mind and stands blotted against the curtain of the door.* MALISE *enters. For a moment he does not see her standing there against the curtain that is much the same colour as her dress. His face is that of a man in the grip of a rage that he feels to be impotent. Then, seeing her, he pulls himself together, walks to his armchair, and sits down there in his hat and coat.*

CLARE. Well? "The Watchfire?" You may as well tell me.

MALISE. Nothing to tell you, child.

> *At that touch of tenderness she goes up to his chair and kneels down beside it. Mechanically* MALISE *takes off his hat.*

CLARE. Then you are to lose that, too? [MALISE *stares at her*] I know about it—never mind how.

MALISE. Sanctimonious dogs!

CLARE. [*Very low*] There are other things to be got, aren't there?

MALISE. Thick as blackberries. I just go out and cry, "Malise, unsuccessful author, too honest journalist, freethinker, co-respondent, bankrupt," and they tumble!

CLARE. [*Quietly*] Kenneth, do you care for me? [MALISE *stares at her*] Am I anything to you but just prettiness?

MALISE. Now, now! This isn't the time to brood! Rouse up and fight.

CLARE. Yes.

MALISE. We're not going to let them down us, are we? [*She rubs her cheek against his hand, that still rests on her shoulder*] Life on sufferance, breath at the pleasure of the enemy! And some day in the fullness of his mercy to be made a present of the right to eat and drink and breathe again. [*His gesture sums up the rage within him*] Fine! [*He puts his hat on and rises*] That's the last groan they get from me.

CLARE. Are you going out again? [*He nods*] Where?

MALISE. Blackberrying! Our train's not till six.

> *He goes into the bedroom. CLARE gets up and stands by the fire, looking round in a dazed way. She puts her hand up and mechanically gathers together the violets in the little vase. Suddenly she twists them to a buttonhole, and sinks down into the armchair, which he must pass. There she sits, the violets in her hand. MALISE comes out and crosses towards the outer door. She puts the violets up to him. He stares at them, shrugs his shoulders, and passes on. For just a moment CLARE sits motionless.*

CLARE. [*Quietly*] Give me a kiss!

> *He turns and kisses her. But his lips, after that kiss, have the furtive bitterness one sees on the lips of those who have done what does not suit their mood. He goes out. She is left motionless by the armchair, her throat working. Then, feverishly, she goes to the little table, seizes a sheet of paper, and writes. Looking up suddenly she sees that MRS. MILER has let herself in with her latchkey.*

MRS. MILER. I've settled the baker, the milk, the washin' an' the groceries—this 'ere's what's left.

> *She counts down a five-pound note, four sovereigns, and two shillings on to the little table. CLARE folds the letter into an envelope, then takes up the five-pound note and puts it into her dress.*

CLARE. [*Pointing to the money on the table*] Take

your wages; and give him this when he comes in. I'm going away.

MRS. MILER. Without him? When'll you be comin' back?

CLARE. [*Rising*] I shan't be coming back. [*Gazing at* MRS. MILER's *hands, which are plaiting at her dress*] I'm leaving Mr. Malise, and shan't see him again. And the suit against us will be withdrawn—the divorce suit—you understand?

MRS. MILER. [*Her face all broken up*] I never meant to say anything to yer.

CLARE. It's not you. I can see for myself. Don't make it harder; help me. Get a cab.

MRS. MILER. [*Disturbed to the heart*] The porter's outside, cleanin' the landin' winder.

CLARE. Tell him to come for my trunk. It is packed. [*She goes into the bedroom.*

MRS. MILER. [*Opening the door—desolately*] Come 'ere!

[*The* PORTER *appears in shirt-sleeves at the door.*

MRS. MILER. The lady wants a cab. Wait and carry 'er trunk down.

CLARE *comes from the bedroom in her hat and coat.*

MRS. MILER. [*To the* PORTER] Now.

They go into the bedroom to get the trunk. CLARE *picks up from the floor the bunch of violets, her fingers play with it as if they did not quite know what it was; and she stands by the armchair very still, while* MRS. MILER *and the* PORTER *pass*

> her with trunk and bag. And even after the
> PORTER *has shouldered the trunk outside, and
> marched away, and* MRS. MILER *has come back
> into the room,* CLARE *still stands there.*

MRS. MILER. [*Pointing to the typewriter*] D'you want
this 'ere, too?

CLARE. Yes.

> MRS. MILER *carries it out. Then, from the door-
> way, gazing at* CLARE *taking her last look, she
> sobs, suddenly. At sound of that sob* CLARE
> *throws up her head.*

CLARE. Don't! It's all right. Good-bye!

> *She walks out and away, not looking back.* MRS.
> MILER *chokes her sobbing into the black stuff
> of her thick old jacket.*

CURTAIN.

ACT IV

Supper-time *in a small room at "The Gascony" on Derby Day. Through the windows of a broad corridor, out of which the door opens, is seen the dark blue of a summer night. The walls are of apricot-gold; the carpets, curtains, lamp-shades, and gilded chairs, of red; the wood-work and screens white; the palms in gilded tubs. A doorway that has no door leads to another small room. One little table behind a screen, and one little table in the open, are set for two persons each. On a serv-ice-table, above which hangs a speaking-tube, are some dishes of hors d'œuvres, a basket of peaches, two bottles of champagne in ice-pails, and a small barrel of oysters in a gilded tub.* Arnaud, *the waiter, slim, dark, quick, his face seamed with a quiet, soft irony, is opening oysters and listening to the robust joy of a distant supper-party, where a man is playing the last bars of:* "Do ye ken John Peel" *on a horn. As the sound dies away, he murmurs:* "Très Joli!" *and opens another oyster. Two Ladies with bare shoulders and large hats pass down the corridor. Their talk is faintly wafted in:* "Well, I never like Derby night! The boys do get so bobbish!" "That horn—vulgar, I call it!"

79

ARNAUD'S eyebrows rise, the corners of his mouth droop. A Lady with bare shoulders, and crimson roses in her hair, comes along the corridor, and stops for a second at the window, for a man to join her. They come through into the room. ARNAUD has sprung to attention, but with: "Let's go in here, shall we?" they pass through into the further room. The MANAGER, a gentleman with neat moustaches, and buttoned into a frock-coat, has appeared, brisk, noiseless, his eyes everywhere; he inspects the peaches.

MANAGER. Four shillin' apiece to-night, see?

ARNAUD. Yes, Sare.

> *From the inner room a young man and his partner have come in. She is dark, almost Spanish-looking; he fair, languid, pale, clean-shaved, slackly smiling, with half-closed eyes—one of those who are bred and dissipated to the point of having lost all save the capacity for hiding their emotions. He speaks in a—*

LANGUID VOICE. Awful row they're kickin' up in there, Mr. Varley. A fellow with a horn.

MANAGER. [*Blandly*] Gaddesdon Hunt, my lord—always have their supper with us, Derby night. Quiet corner here, my lord. Arnaud!

> *ARNAUD is already at the table, between screen and palm. And, there ensconced, the couple take their seats. Seeing them safely landed, the MANAGER, brisk and noiseless, moves away. In the corridor a lady in black, with a cloak fall-*

> *ing open, seems uncertain whether to come in.*
> *She advances into the doorway. It is* CLARE.

ARNAUD. [*Pointing to the other table as he flies with dishes*] Nice table, Madame.

> CLARE *moves to the corner of it. An artist in observation of his clients,* ARNAUD *takes in her face—very pale under her wavy, simply-dressed hair; shadowy beneath the eyes; not powdered; her lips not reddened; without a single ornament; takes in her black dress, finely cut, her arms and neck beautifully white, and at her breast three gardenias. And as he nears her, she lifts her eyes. It is very much the look of something lost, appealing for guidance.*

ARNAUD. Madame is waiting for some one? [*She shakes her head*] Then Madame will be veree well here— veree well. I take Madame's cloak?

> *He takes the cloak gently and lays it on the back of the chair fronting the room, that she may put it round her when she wishes. She sits down.*

LANGUID VOICE. [*From the corner*] Waiter!

ARNAUD. Milord!

LANGUID VOICE. The Roederer.

ARNAUD. At once, milord.

> CLARE *sits tracing a pattern with her finger on the cloth, her eyes lowered. Once she raises them, and follows* ARNAUD'S *dark rapid figure.*

ARNAUD. [*Returning*] Madame feels the 'eat? [*He scans her with increased curiosity*] You wish something, Madame?

CLARE. [*Again giving him that look*] Must I order?

ARNAUD. Non, Madame, it is not necessary. A glass of water. [*He pours it out*] I have not the pleasure of knowing Madame's face.

CLARE. [*Faintly smiling*] No.

ARNAUD. Madame will find it veree good 'ere, veree quiet.

LANGUID VOICE. Waiter!

ARNAUD. Pardon!   [*He goes.*

> *The bare-necked ladies with large hats again pass down the corridor outside, and again their voices are wafted in:* "Tottie! Not she! Oh! my goodness, she has got a pride on her!" "Bobbie'll never stick it!" "Look here, dear——" *Galvanized by those sounds,* CLARE *has caught her cloak and half-risen; they die away and she subsides.*

ARNAUD. [*Back at her table, with a quaint shrug towards the corridor*] It is not rowdy here, Madame, as a rule—not as in some places. To-night a little noise. Madame is fond of flowers? [*He whisks out, and returns almost at once with a bowl of carnations from some table in the next room*] These smell good!

CLARE. You are very kind.

ARNAUD. [*With courtesy*] Not at all, Madame; a pleasure.   [*He bows.*

> *A young man, tall, thin, hard, straight, with close-cropped, sandyish hair and moustache, a face tanned very red, and one of those small, long, lean heads that only grow in Britain;*

*clad in a thin dark overcoat thrown open, an
opera hat pushed back, a white waistcoat round
his lean middle, he comes in from the corridor.
He looks round, glances at* CLARE, *passes her
table towards the further room, stops in the doorway, and looks back at her. Her eyes have just
been lifted, and are at once cast down again.
The young man wavers, catches* ARNAUD'S *eye,
jerks his head to summon him, and passes into
the further room.* ARNAUD *takes up the vase
that has been superseded, and follows him out.
And* CLARE *sits alone in silence, broken by the
murmurs of the languid lord and his partner,
behind the screen. She is breathing as if she
had been running hard. She lifts her eyes.
The tall young man, divested of hat and coat,
is standing by her table, holding out his hand
with a sort of bashful hardiness.*

YOUNG MAN. How d'you do? Didn't recognize you
at first. So sorry—awfully rude of me.

CLARE'S *eyes seem to fly from him, to appeal to
him, to resign herself all at once. Something in
the* YOUNG MAN *responds. He drops his hand.*

CLARE. [*Faintly*] How d'you do?

YOUNG MAN. [*Stammering*] You—you been down
there to-day?

CLARE. Where?

YOUNG MAN. [*With a smile*] The Derby. What?
Don't you generally go down? [*He touches the other
chair*] May I?

CLARE. [*Almost in a whisper*] Yes.

> As he sits down, ARNAUD *returns and stands before them.*

ARNAUD. The plovers' eggs veree good to-night, Sare. Veree good, Madame. A peach or two, after. Veree good peaches. The Roederer, Sare—not bad at all. Madame likes it *frappé*, but not too cold—yes?

> [*He is away again to his service-table.*

YOUNG MAN. [*Burying his face in the carnations*] I say—these are jolly, aren't they? They do you pretty well here.

CLARE. Do they?

YOUNG MAN. You've never been here? [CLARE *shakes her head*] By Jove! I thought I didn't know your face. [CLARE *looks full at him. Again something moves in the* YOUNG MAN, *and he stammers*] I mean—not——

CLARE. It doesn't matter.

YOUNG MAN. [*Respectfully*] Of course, if I—if you were waiting for anybody, or anything—I——

> [*He half rises.*

CLARE. It's all right, thank you.

> The YOUNG MAN *sits down again, uncomfortable, nonplussed. There is silence, broken by the inaudible words of the languid lord, and the distant merriment of the supper-party.* ARNAUD *brings the plovers' eggs.*

YOUNG MAN. The wine, quick.

ARNAUD. At once, Sare.

YOUNG MAN. [*Abruptly*] Don't you ever go racing, then?

CLARE. No.

> [ARNAUD *pours out champagne.*

YOUNG MAN. I remember awfully well my first day. It was pretty thick—lost every blessed bob, and my watch and chain, playin' three cards on the way home.

CLARE. Everything has a beginning, hasn't it?

> [*She drinks. The* YOUNG MAN *stares at her.*

YOUNG MAN. [*Floundering in these waters deeper than he had bargained for*] I say—about things having beginnings—did you mean anything?

> [CLARE *nods.*

YOUNG MAN. What! D'you mean it's really the first——?

> CLARE *nods. The champagne has flicked her*
> *courage.*

YOUNG MAN. By George! [*He leans back*] I've often wondered.

ARNAUD. [*Again filling the glasses*] Monsieur finds——

YOUNG MAN. [*Abruptly*] It's all right.

> *He drains his glass, then sits bolt upright. Chiv-*
> *alry and the camaraderie of class have begun to*
> *stir in him.*

YOUNG MAN. Of course I can see that you're not —I mean, that you're a—a lady. [CLARE *smiles*] And I say, you know—if you have to—because you're in a hole—I should feel a cad. Let me lend you——?

CLARE. [*Holding up her glass*] *Le vin est tiré, il faut le boire!*

> *She drinks. The French words, which he does not too well understand, completing his conviction that she is a lady, he remains quite silent, frowning. As* CLARE *held up her glass, two gentlemen have entered. The first is blond, of good height and a comely insolence. His crisp, fair hair, and fair brushed-up moustache are just going grey; an eyeglass is fixed in one of two eyes that lord it over every woman they see; his face is broad, and coloured with air and wine. His companion is a tall, thin, dark bird of the night, with sly, roving eyes, and hollow cheeks. They stand looking round, then pass into the further room; but in passing, they have stared unreservedly at* CLARE.

YOUNG MAN. [*Seeing her wince*] Look here! I'm afraid you must feel me rather a brute, you know.

CLARE. No, I don't; really.

YOUNG MAN. Are you absolute stoney? [CLARE nods] But [*Looking at her frock and cloak*] you're so awfully well——

CLARE. I had the sense to keep them.

YOUNG MAN. [*More and more disturbed*] I say, you know—I wish you'd let me lend you something. I had quite a good day down there.

CLARE. [*Again tracing her pattern on the cloth—then looking up at him full*] I can't take, for nothing.

YOUNG MAN. By Jove! I don't know—really, I

don't—this makes me feel pretty rotten. I mean, it's your being a lady.

CLARE. [*Smiling*] That's not your fault, is it? You see, I've been beaten all along the line. And I really don't care what happens to me. [*She has that peculiar fey look on her face now*] I really don't; except that I don't take charity. It's lucky for me it's you, and not some——

> *The supper-party is getting still more boisterous, and there comes a long view holloa, and a blast of the horn.*

YOUNG MAN. But I say, what about your people? You must have people of some sort.

> *He is fast becoming fascinated, for her cheeks have begun to flush and her eyes to shine.*

CLARE. Oh, yes; I've had people, and a husband, and —everything—— And here I am! Queer, isn't it? [*She touches her glass*] This is going to my head! Do you mind? I sha'n't sing songs and get up and dance, and I won't cry, I promise you!

YOUNG MAN. [*Between fascination and chivalry*] By George! One simply can't believe in this happening to a lady——

CLARE. Have you got sisters? [*Breaking into her soft laughter*] *My* brother's in India. I sha'n't meet *him*, anyway.

YOUNG MAN. No, but—I say—are you really quite cut off from everybody? [CLARE *nods*] Something rather awful must have happened?

> *She smiles. The two gentlemen have returned.*

The blond one is again staring fixedly at CLARE.
*This time she looks back at him, flaming; and,
with a little laugh, he passes with his friend into
the corridor.*

CLARE. Who are those two?

YOUNG MAN. Don't know—not been much about
town yet. I'm just back from India myself. You said
your brother was there; what's his regiment?

CLARE. [*Shaking her head*] You're not going to find
out my name. I haven't got one—nothing.

*She leans her bare elbows on the table, and her
face on her hands.*

CLARE. First of June! This day last year I broke
covert—I've been running ever since.

YOUNG MAN. I don't understand a bit. You—
must have had a—a—some one——

*But there is such a change in her face, such rigid-
ity of her whole body, that he stops and averts
his eyes. When he looks again she is drinking.
She puts the glass down, and gives a little laugh.*

YOUNG MAN. [*With a sort of awe*] Anyway it must
have been like riding at a pretty stiff fence, for you to
come here to-night.

CLARE. Yes. What's the other side?

The YOUNG MAN *puts out his hand and touches
her arm. It is meant for sympathy, but she
takes it for attraction.*

CLARE. [*Shaking her head*] Not yet—please! I'm
enjoying this. May I have a cigarette?

[*He takes out his case, and gives her one.*

CLARE. [*Letting the smoke slowly forth*] Yes, I'm enjoying it. Had a pretty poor time lately; not enough to eat, sometimes.

YOUNG MAN. Not really! How damnable! I say —do have something more substantial.

    CLARE *gives a sudden gasp, as if going off into hysterical laughter, but she stifles it, and shakes her head.*

YOUNG MAN. A peach?

    [ARNAUD *brings peaches to the table.*

CLARE. [*Smiling*] Thank you.

    [*He fills their glasses and retreats.*

CLARE. [*Raising her glass*] Eat and drink, for to-morrow we—Listen!

    From the supper-party comes the sound of an abortive chorus: "With a hey ho, chivy, hark forrard, hark forrard, tantivy!" *Jarring out into a discordant whoop, it sinks.*

CLARE. "This day a stag must die." Jolly old song!

YOUNG MAN. Rowdy lot! [*Suddenly*] I say—I admire your pluck.

CLARE. [*Shaking her head*] Haven't kept my end up. Lots of women do! You see: I'm too fine, and not fine enough! My best friend said that. Too fine, and not fine enough. [*She laughs*] I couldn't be a saint and martyr, and I wouldn't be a soulless doll. Neither one thing nor the other—that's the tragedy.

YOUNG MAN. You must have had awful luck!

CLARE. I *did* try. [*Fiercely*] But what's the good—when there's nothing before you?—Do I look ill?

YOUNG MAN. No; simply awfully pretty.

CLARE. [*With a laugh*] A man once said to me: "As you haven't money, you should never have been pretty!" But, you see, it is some good. If I hadn't been, I couldn't have risked coming here, could I? Don't you think it was rather sporting of me to buy these [*She touches the gardenias*] with the last shilling over from my cab fare?

YOUNG MAN. Did you really? D——d sporting!

CLARE. It's no use doing things by halves, is it? I'm—in for it—wish me luck! [*She drinks, and puts her glass down with a smile*] In for it—deep! [*She flings up her hands above her smiling face*] Down, down, till they're just above water, and then—down, down, down, and—all over! Are you sorry now you came and spoke to me?

YOUNG MAN. By Jove, no! It may be caddish, but I'm not.

CLARE. Thank God for beauty! I hope I shall die pretty! Do you think I shall *do* well?

YOUNG MAN. I say—*don't* talk like that!

CLARE. I want to know. *Do* you?

YOUNG MAN. Well, then—yes, I do.

CLARE. That's splendid. Those poor women in the streets would give their eyes, wouldn't they?—that have to go up and down, up and down! Do you think I—shall——

> The YOUNG MAN, *half-rising, puts his hand on her arm.*

YOUNG MAN. I think you're getting much too ex-

cited. You look all—Won't you eat your peach?
[*She shakes her head*] Do! Have something else, then
—some grapes, or something?

CLARE. No, thanks.

[*She has become quite calm again.*

YOUNG MAN. Well, then, what d'you think? It's
awfully hot in here, isn't it? Wouldn't it be jollier
drivin'? Shall we—shall we make a move?

CLARE. Yes.

The YOUNG MAN *turns to look for the waiter,
but* ARNAUD *is not in the room. He gets up.*

YOUNG MAN. [*Feverishly*] D——n that waiter! Wait
half a minute, if you don't mind, while I pay the bill.

*As he goes out into the corridor, the two gentlemen
re-appear.* CLARE *is sitting motionless, looking straight before her.*

DARK ONE. A fiver you don't get her to!

BLOND ONE. Done!

*He advances to her table with his inimitable inso-
lence, and taking the cigar from his mouth,
bends his stare on her, and says:* "Charmed to
see you lookin' so well! Will you have supper with me here to-morrow night?" *Startled
out of her reverie,* CLARE *looks up. She sees
those eyes, she sees beyond him the eyes of his
companion—sly, malevolent, amused—watching; and she just sits gazing, without a word.
At that regard, so clear, the* BLOND ONE *does not
wince. But rather suddenly he says:* "That's
arranged then. Half-past eleven. So good
of you. Good-night!" *He replaces his cigar*

*and strolls back to his companion, and in a low
voice says:* "Pay up!" *Then at a languid*
"Hullo, Charles!" *they turn to greet the two in
their nook behind the screen.* CLARE *has not
moved, nor changed the direction of her gaze.
Suddenly she thrusts her hand into the pocket
of the cloak that hangs behind her, and brings
out the little blue bottle which, six months ago,
she took from* MALISE. *She pulls out the cork
and pours the whole contents into her champagne.
She lifts the glass, holds it before her—smiling,
as if to call a toast, then puts it to her lips and
drinks. Still smiling, she sets the empty glass
down, and lays the gardenia flowers against
her face. Slowly she droops back in her chair,
the drowsy smile still on her lips; the gardenias
drop into her lap; her arms relax, her head falls
forward on her breast. And the voices behind
the screen talk on, and the sounds of joy from the
supper-party wax and wane.*

The waiter, ARNAUD, *returning from the corridor,
passes to his service-table with a tall, be-rib-
boned basket of fruit. Putting it down, he goes
towards the table behind the screen, and sees.
He runs up to* CLARE.

ARNAUD. Madame! Madame! [*He listens for her
breathing; then suddenly catching sight of the little bottle,
smells at it*] Bon Dieu!

*At that queer sound they come from behind the screen
—all four, and look. The dark night bird says:*
"Hallo; fainted!" ARNAUD *holds out the bottle.*

LANGUID LORD. [*Taking it, and smelling*] Good God!
    The woman bends over CLARE, *and lifts her hands;*
    ARNAUD *rushes to his service-table, and speaks*
    into his tube:

ARNAUD. The boss.   Quick! [*Looking up he sees the*
YOUNG MAN, *returning*] Monsieur, elle a fui !   Elle est
morte !

LANGUID LORD. [*To the* YOUNG MAN *standing there
aghast*] What's this?   Friend of yours?

YOUNG MAN. My God!   She was a lady.   That's
all I know about her.

LANGUID LORD. A lady!

    *The blond and dark gentlemen have slipped from
    the room; and out of the supper-party's distant
    laughter comes suddenly a long, shrill:* "Gone
    away!"   *And the sound of the horn playing
    the seven last notes of the old song:* "This day a
    stag must die!"   *From the last note of all the
    sound flies up to an octave higher, sweet and
    thin, like a spirit passing, till it is drowned
    once more in laughter.   The* YOUNG MAN *has
    covered his eyes with his hands;* ARNAUD *is
    crossing himself fervently; the* LANGUID LORD
    stands gazing, with one of the dropped gardenias
    twisted in his fingers; and the woman, bending
    over* CLARE, *kisses her forehead.*

CURTAIN.

THE PIGEON

A FANTASY IN THREE ACTS

PERSONS OF THE PLAY

CHRISTOPHER WELLWYN, *an artist*
ANN, *his daughter*
GUINEVERE MEGAN, *a flower-seller*
RORY MEGAN, *her husband*
FERRAND, *an alien*
TIMSON, *once a cabman*
EDWARD BERTLEY, *a Canon*
ALFRED CALWAY, *a Professor*
SIR THOMAS HOXTON, *a Justice of the Peace*
*Also a police constable, three humble-men, and some
    curious persons*

The action passes in Wellwyn's Studio, and the street outside.

ACT   I. *Christmas Eve.*
ACT II. *New Year's Day.*
ACT III. *The First of April.*

CAST OF THE FIRST PRODUCTION

BY

MESSRS. J. E. VEDRENNE AND DENNIS EADIE

AT THE

ROYALTY THEATRE, LONDON, ON JANUARY 30TH, 1912

CHRISTOPHER WELLWYN	MR. WHITFORD KANE
ANN	MISS GLADYS COOPER
FERRAND	MR. DENNIS EADIE
TIMSON	MR. WILFRED SHINE
MRS. MEGAN	MISS MARGARET MORRIS
MEGAN	MR. STANLEY LOGAN
CANON BERTLEY	MR. HUBERT HARBEN
PROFESSOR CALWAY	MR. FRANK VERNON
SIR THOMAS HOXTON	MR. FREDERICK LLOYD
POLICE CONSTABLE	MR. ARTHUR B. MURRAY
FIRST HUMBLE-MAN	MR. W. LEMMON WARDE
SECOND HUMBLE-MAN	MR. F. B. J. SHARP
THIRD HUMBLE-MAN	MR. ARTHUR BOWYER
A LOAFER	MR. ARTHUR BAXENDELL

ACT I

It is the night of Christmas Eve, the SCENE *is a Studio, flush with the street, having a skylight darkened by a fall of snow. There is no one in the room, the walls of which are whitewashed, above a floor of bare dark boards. A fire is cheerfully burning. On a model's platform stands an easel and canvas. There are busts and pictures; a screen, a little stool, two arm-chairs, and a long old-fashioned settle under the window. A door in one wall leads to the house, a door in the opposite wall to the model's dressing-room, and the street door is in the centre of the wall between. On a low table a Russian samovar is hissing, and beside it on a tray stands a teapot, with glasses, lemon, sugar, and a decanter of rum. Through a huge uncurtained window close to the street door the snowy lamplit street can be seen, and beyond it the river and a night of stars.*

The sound of a latchkey turned in the lock of the street door, and ANN WELLWYN *enters, a girl of seventeen, with hair tied in a ribbon and covered by a scarf. Leaving the door open, she turns up the electric light and goes to the fire. She throws off her scarf and long red cloak. She is dressed in a high evening frock of some soft white material. Her movements*

1

are quick and substantial.   Her face, full of no non-
sense, is decided and sincere, with deep-set eyes, and
a capable, well-shaped forehead.   Shredding off her
gloves she warms her hands.

In the doorway appear the figures of two men.   The first
is rather short and slight, with a soft short beard,
bright soft eyes, and a crumply face.   Under his
squash hat his hair is rather plentiful and rather
grey.   He wears an old brown ulster and woollen
gloves, and is puffing at a hand-made cigarette.   He
is ANN's father, WELLWYN, the artist.   His com-
panion is a well-wrapped clergyman of medium
height and stoutish build, with a pleasant, rosy face,
rather shining eyes, and rather chubby clean-shaped
lips; in appearance, indeed, a grown-up boy.   He
is the Vicar of the parish—CANON BERTLEY.

BERTLEY. My dear Wellwyn, the whole question of
reform is full of difficulty.   When you have two men
like Professor Calway and Sir Thomas Hoxton taking
diametrically opposite points of view, as we've seen
to-night, I confess, I——

WELLWYN. Come in, Vicar, and have some grog.

BERTLEY. Not to-night, thanks!   Christmas to-
morrow!   Great temptation, though, this room!   Good-
night, Wellwyn; good-night, Ann!

ANN. [*Coming from the fire towards the tea-table.*]
Good-night, Canon Bertley.

> [*He goes out, and* WELLWYN, *shutting the door*
> *after him, approaches the fire.*

ANN. [*Sitting on the little stool, with her back to the fire, and making tea.*] Daddy!

WELLWYN. My dear?

ANN. You say you liked Professor Calway's lecture. Is it going to do you any good, that's the question?

WELLWYN. I—I hope so, Ann.

ANN. I took you on purpose. Your charity's getting simply awful. Those two this morning cleared out all my housekeeping money.

WELLWYN. Um! Um! I quite understand your feeling.

ANN. They both had your card, so I couldn't refuse —didn't know what you'd said to them. Why don't you make it a rule never to give your card to anyone except really decent people, and—picture dealers, of course.

WELLWYN. My dear, I have—often.

ANN. Then why don't you keep it? It's a frightful habit. You *are* naughty, Daddy. One of these days you'll get yourself into most fearful complications.

WELLWYN. My dear, when they—when they look at you?

ANN. You know the house wants all sorts of things. Why do you speak to them at all?

WELLWYN. I don't—they speak to me.

[*He takes off his ulster and hangs it over the back of an arm-chair.*

ANN. They see you coming. Anybody can see *you* coming, Daddy. That's why you ought to be so careful. I shall make you wear a hard hat. Those squashy hats of yours are hopelessly inefficient.

WELLWYN. [*Gazing at his hat.*] Calway wears one.

ANN. As if anyone would beg of Professor Calway.

WELLWYN. Well—perhaps not. You know, Ann, I admire that fellow. Wonderful power of—of—theory! How a man can be so absolutely tidy in his mind! It's most exciting.

ANN. Has any one begged of you to-day?

WELLWYN. [*Doubtfully.*] No—no.

ANN. [*After a long, severe look.*] Will you have rum in your tea?

WELLWYN. [*Crestfallen.*] Yes, my dear—a good deal.

ANN. [*Pouring out the rum, and handing him the glass.*] Well, who was it?

WELLWYN. He didn't beg of me. [*Losing himself in recollection.*] Interesting old creature, Ann—real type. Old cabman.

ANN. Where?

WELLWYN. Just on the Embankment.

ANN. Of course! Daddy, you know the Embankment ones are *always* rotters.

WELLWYN. Yes, my dear; but this wasn't.

ANN. Did you give him your card?

WELLWYN. I—I—don't——

ANN. *Did* you, Daddy?

WELLWYN. I'm rather afraid I may have!

ANN. May have! It's simply immoral.

WELLWYN. Well, the old fellow was so awfully human, Ann. Besides, I didn't give him any money—hadn't got any.

ANN. Look here, Daddy! Did you ever ask anybody for anything? You know you never did, you'd starve first. So would anybody decent. Then, why won't you see that people who beg are rotters?

WELLWYN. But, my dear, we're not all the same. They wouldn't do it if it wasn't natural to them. One likes to be friendly. What's the use of being alive if one isn't?

ANN. Daddy, you're hopeless.

WELLWYN. But, look here, Ann, the whole thing's so jolly complicated. According to Calway, we're to give the State all we can spare, to make the undeserving deserving. He's a Professor; he ought to know. But old Hoxton's always dinning it into me that we ought to support private organisations for helping the deserving, and damn the undeserving. Well, that's just the opposite. And he's a J.P. Tremendous experience. And the Vicar seems to be for a little bit of both. Well, what the devil—? My trouble is, whichever I'm with, he always converts me. [*Ruefully.*] And there's no fun in any of them.

ANN. [*Rising.*] Oh! Daddy, you are so—don't you know that you're the despair of all social reformers? [*She envelops him.*] There's a tear in the left knee of your trousers. You're not to wear them again.

WELLWYN. Am I likely to?

ANN. I shouldn't be a bit surprised if it isn't your only pair. D'you know what I live in terror of?

[WELLWYN *gives her a queer and apprehensive look.*

ANN. That you'll take them off some day, and give them away in the street. Have you got any money? [*She feels in his coat, and he is his trousers—they find nothing.*] Do you know that your pockets are one enormous hole?

WELLWYN. No!

ANN. Spiritually.

WELLWYN. Oh! Ah! H'm!

ANN. [*Severely.*] Now, look here, Daddy! [*She takes him by his lappels.*] Don't imagine that it isn't the most disgusting luxury on your part to go on giving away things as you do! You know what you really are, I suppose—a sickly sentimentalist!

WELLWYN. [*Breaking away from her, disturbed.*] It isn't sentiment. It's simply that they seem to me so—so—jolly. If I'm to give up feeling sort of —nice in here [*he touches his chest*] about people—it doesn't matter *who* they are—then I don't know what I'm to do. I shall have to sit with my head in a bag.

ANN. I think you ought to.

WELLWYN. I suppose they see I like them—then they tell me things. After that, of course you can't help doing what you can.

ANN. Well, if you *will* love them up!

WELLWYN. My dear, I don't want to. It isn't *them* especially—why, I feel it even with old Calway sometimes. It's only Providence that he doesn't want anything of me—except to make me like himself—confound him!

ANN. [*Moving towards the door into the house—impressively.*] What you don't see is that other people aren't a bit like *you*.

WELLWYN. Well, thank God!

ANN. It's so old-fashioned too! I'm going to bed— I just leave you to your conscience.

WELLWYN. Oh!

ANN. [*Opening the door—severely.*] Good-night— [*with a certain weakening*] you old—Daddy!

> [*She jumps at him, gives him a hug, and goes out.*
>
> [WELLWYN *stands perfectly still. He first gazes up at the skylight, then down at the floor. Slowly he begins to shake his head, and mutter, as he moves towards the fire.*

WELLWYN. Bad lot. . . . Low type—no backbone, no stability!

> [*There comes a fluttering knock on the outer door. As the sound slowly enters his consciousness, he begins to wince, as though he knew, but would not admit its significance. Then he sits down, covering his ears. The knocking does not cease.* WELLWYN *drops first one, then both hands, rises, and begins to sidle towards the door. The knocking becomes louder.*

WELLWYN. Ah dear! Tt! Tt! Tt!

> [*After a look in the direction of* ANN'S *disappearance, he opens the street door a very little way. By the light of the lamp there can be seen a young girl in dark clothes, huddled in a shawl to which*

the snow is clinging.   She has on her arm a bas-
ket covered with a bit of sacking.

WELLWYN. I can't, you know; it's impossible.

[*The girl says nothing, but looks at him with dark*
eyes.

WELLWYN. [*Wincing.*] Let's see—I don't know you
—do I?

[*The girl, speaking in a soft, hoarse voice, with a*
faint accent of reproach: "Mrs. Megan—you
give me this—"   *She holds out a dirty visiting*
card.

WELLWYN. [*Recoiling from the card.*] Oh! Did I?
Ah! When?

MRS. MEGAN. You 'ad some vi'lets off of me larst
spring. You give me 'arf a crown.

[*A smile tries to visit her face.*

WELLWYN. [*Looking   stealthily   round.*] Ah! Well,
come in—just for a minute—it's very cold—and tell us
what it is.

[*She comes in stolidly, a sphinx-like figure, with*
her pretty tragic little face.

WELLWYN. I don't remember you. [*Looking closer.*]
Yes, *I* do. Only—you weren't the same—were you?

MRS. MEGAN. [*Dully.*] I seen trouble since.

WELLWYN. Trouble! Have some tea?

[*He looks anxiously at the door into the house, then*
goes quickly to the table, and pours out a glass of
tea, putting rum into it.

WELLWYN. [*Handing her the tea.*] Keeps the cold out!
Drink it off!

[MRS. MEGAN *drinks it off, chokes a little, and almost immediately seems to get a size larger.* WELLWYN *watches her with his head held on one side, and a smile broadening on his face.*

WELLWYN. Cure for all evils, um?

MRS. MEGAN. It warms you.   [*She smiles.*

WELLWYN. [*Smiling back, and catching himself out.*] Well! You know, I oughtn't.

MRS. MEGAN. [*Conscious of the disruption of his personality, and withdrawing into her tragic abyss.*] I wouldn't 'a come, but you told me if I wanted an 'and——

WELLWYN. [*Gradually losing himself in his own nature.*] Let me see—corner of Flight Street, wasn't it?

MRS. MEGAN. [*With faint eagerness.*] Yes, sir, an' I told you about me vi'lets—it was a luvly spring day.

WELLWYN. Beautiful! Beautiful! Birds singing, and the trees, &c.! We had quite a talk. You had a baby with you.

MRS. MEGAN. Yes. I got married since then.

WELLWYN. Oh! Ah! Yes! [*Cheerfully.*] And how's the baby?

MRS. MEGAN. [*Turning to stone.*] I lost her.

WELLWYN. Oh! poor— Um!

MRS. MEGAN. [*Impassive.*] You said something abaht makin' a picture of me. [*With faint eagerness.*] So I thought I might come, in case you'd forgotten.

WELLWYN. [*Looking at her intently.*] Things going badly?

MRS. MEGAN. [*Stripping the sacking off her basket.*]
I keep 'em covered up, but the cold gets to 'em.
Thruppence—that's all I've took.

WELLWYN. Ho! Tt! Tt! [*He looks into the basket.*]
Christmas, too!

MRS. MEGAN. They're dead.

WELLWYN. [*Drawing in his breath.*] Got a *good* husband?

MRS. MEGAN. He plays cards.

WELLWYN. Oh, Lord! And what are you doing out
—with a cold like that? [*He taps his chest.*

MRS. MEGAN. We was sold up this morning—he's
gone off with 'is mates. Haven't took enough yet for
a night's lodgin'.

WELLWYN. [*Correcting a spasmodic dive into his
pockets.*] But who buys *flowers* at this time of night?

[MRS. MEGAN *looks at him, and faintly smiles.*

WELLWYN. [*Rumpling his hair.*] Saints above us!
Here! Come to the fire!

[*She follows him to the fire. He shuts the street
door.*

WELLWYN. Are your feet wet? [*She nods.*] Well, sit
down here, and take them off. That's right.

[*She sits on the stool. And after a slow look up at
him, which has in it a deeper knowledge than
belongs of right to her years, begins taking off
her shoes and stockings. WELLWYN goes to the
door into the house, opens it, and listens with a
sort of stealthy casualness. He returns whis-
tling, but not out loud. The girl has finished tak-*

*ing off her stockings, and turned her bare toes
to the flames. She shuffles them back under her
skirt.*

WELLWYN. How old are you, my child?

MRS. MEGAN. Nineteen, come Candlemas.

WELLWYN. And what's your name?

MRS. MEGAN. Guinevere.

WELLWYN. What? Welsh?

MRS. MEGAN. Yes—from Battersea.

WELLWYN. And your husband?

MRS. MEGAN. No. Irish, 'e is. Notting Dale, 'e
comes from.

WELLWYN. Roman Catholic?

MRS. MEGAN. Yes. My 'usband's an atheist as
well.

WELLWYN. I see. [*Abstractedly.*] How jolly! And
how old is he—this young man of yours?

MRS. MEGAN. 'E'll be twenty soon.

WELLWYN. Babes in the wood! Does he treat you
badly?

MRS. MEGAN. No.

WELLWYN. Nor drink?

MRS. MEGAN. No. He's not a bad one. Only he
gets playin' cards—then 'e'll fly the kite.

WELLWYN. I see. And when he's not flying it, what
does he do?

MRS. MEGAN. [*Touching her basket.*] Same as me.
Other jobs tires 'im.

WELLWYN. That's very nice! [*He checks himself.*]
Well, what am I to do with you?

MRS. MEGAN. Of course, I could get me night's lodging if I like to do—the same as some of them.

WELLWYN. No! no! Never, my child! Never!

MRS. MEGAN. It's easy that way.

WELLWYN. Heavens! But your husband! Um?

MRS. MEGAN. [*With stoical vindictiveness.*] He's after one I know of.

WELLWYN. Tt! What a pickle!

MRS. MEGAN. I'll 'ave to walk about the streets.

WELLWYN. [*To himself.*] Now how can I?

　　　　[MRS. MEGAN *looks up and smiles at him, as if she had already discovered that he is peculiar.*

WELLWYN. You see, the fact is, I mustn't give you anything—because—well, for one thing I haven't got it. There are other reasons, but that's the—real one. But, now, there's a little room where my models dress. I wonder if you could sleep there. Come, and see.

　　　　[*The Girl gets up lingeringly, loth to leave the warmth. She takes up her wet stockings.*

MRS. MEGAN. Shall I put them on again?

WELLWYN. No, no; there's a nice warm pair of slippers. [*Seeing the steam rising from her.*] Why, you're wet all over. Here, wait a little!

　　　　[*He crosses to the door into the house, and after stealthy listening, steps through. The Girl, like a cat, steals back to the warmth of the fire.* WELLWYN *returns with a candle, a canary-coloured bath gown, and two blankets.*

WELLWYN. Now then! [*He precedes her towards the door of the model's room.*] Hsssh! [*He opens the door and*

holds up the candle to show her the room.] Will it do?
There's a couch. You'll find some washing things.
Make yourself quite at home. See!

> [*The Girl, perfectly dumb, passes through with her
> basket—and her shoes and stockings.* WELLWYN
> *hands her the candle, blankets, and bath gown.*

WELLWYN. Have a good sleep, child! Forget that
you're alive! [*He closes the door, mournfully.*] Done it
again! [*He goes to the table, cuts a large slice of cake,
knocks on the door, and hands it in.*] Chow-chow!
[*Then, as he walks away, he sights the opposite door.*]
Well—damn it, what *could* I have done? Not a far-
thing on me! [*He goes to the street door to shut it, but first
opens it wide to confirm himself in his hospitality.*] Night
like this!

> [*A sputter of snow is blown in his face.   A voice
> says:* "Monsieur, pardon!" WELLWYN *re-
> coils spasmodically.   A figure moves from the
> lamp-post to the doorway.   He is seen to be
> young and to have ragged clothes.   He speaks
> again:* "You do not remember me, Monsieur?
> My name is Ferrand—it was in Paris, in
> the Champs-Elysées—by the fountain. . . .
> When you came to the door, Monsieur—I am
> not made of iron. . . . Tenez, here is your
> card—I have never lost it." *He holds out to*
> WELLWYN *an old and dirty visiting card.   As
> inch by inch he has advanced into the doorway,
> the light from within falls on him, a tall gaunt
> young pagan with fair hair and reddish golden*

stubble of beard, a long ironical nose a little to one
side, and large, grey, rather prominent eyes.
There is a certain grace in his figure and move-
ments; his clothes are nearly dropping off him.

WELLWYN. [*Yielding to a pleasant memory.*] Ah! yes.
By the fountain. I was sitting there, and you came
and ate a roll, and drank the water.

FERRAND. [*With faint eagerness.*] My breakfast. I
was in poverty—veree bad off. You gave me ten francs.
I thought I had a little the right [WELLWYN *makes a*
movement of disconcertion], seeing you said that if I came
to England——

WELLWYN. Um! And so you've come?

FERRAND. It was time that I consolidated my for-
tunes, Monsieur.

WELLWYN. And you—have——

[*He stops embarrassed.*

FERRAND. [*Shrugging his ragged shoulders.*] One is
not yet Rothschild.

WELLWYN. [*Sympathetically.*] No. [*Yielding to mem-*
ory.] We talked philosophy.

FERRAND. I have not yet changed my opinion. We
other vagabonds, we are exploited by the bourgeois.
This is always my idea, Monsieur.

WELLWYN. Yes—not quite the general view, perhaps! Well— [*Heartily.*] Come in! Very glad to see
you again.

FERRAND. [*Brushing his arms over his eyes.*] Pardon,
Monsieur—your goodness—I am a little weak. [*He*
opens his coat, and shows a belt drawn very tight over his

ragged shirt.] I tighten him one hole for each meal, during two days now. That gives you courage.

WELLWYN. [*With cooing sounds, pouring out tea, and adding rum.*] Have some of this. It'll buck you up.
[*He watches the young man drink.*

FERRAND. [*Becoming a size larger.*] Sometimes I think that I will never succeed to dominate my life, Monsieur—though I have no vices, except that I guard always the aspiration to achieve success. But I will not roll myself under the machine of existence to gain a nothing every day. I must find with what to fly a little.

WELLWYN. [*Delicately.*] Yes; yes—I remember, you found it difficult to stay long in any particular—yes.

FERRAND. [*Proudly.*] In one little corner? No—Monsieur—never! That is not in my character. I must see life.

WELLWYN. Quite, quite! Have some cake?
[*He cuts cake.*

FERRAND. In your country they say you cannot eat the cake and have it. But one must always try, Monsieur; one must never be content. [*Refusing the cake.*] *Grand merci*, but for the moment I have no stomach—I have lost my stomach now for two days. If I could smoke, Monsieur! [*He makes the gesture of smoking.*

WELLWYN. Rather! [*Handing his tobacco pouch.*] Roll yourself one.

FERRAND. [*Rapidly rolling a cigarette.*] If I had not found you, Monsieur—I would have been a little hole in the river to-night—I was so discouraged. [*He inhales and puffs a long luxurious whiff of smoke. Very bitterly.*]

Life! [*He disperses the puff of smoke with his finger, and stares before him.*] And to think that in a few minutes HE will be born! Monsieur! [*He gazes intently at* WELL-WYN.] The world would reproach you for your goodness to me.

WELLWYN. [*Looking uneasily at the door into the house.*] You think so? Ah!

FERRAND. Monsieur, if HE himself were on earth now, there would be a little heap of gentlemen writing to the journals every day to call Him sloppee senti-mentalist! And what is veree funny, these gentlemen they would all be most strong Christians. [*He regards* WELLWYN *deeply.*] But that will not trouble you, Monsieur; I saw well from the first that you are no Christian. You have so kind a face.

WELLWYN. Oh! Indeed!

FERRAND. You have not enough the Pharisee in your character. You do not judge, and you are judged.

[*He stretches his limbs as if in pain.*

WELLWYN. Are you in pain?

FERRAND. I 'ave a little the rheumatism

WELLWYN. Wet through, of course! [*Glancing tow-ards the house.*] Wait a bit! I wonder if you'd like these trousers; they've—er—they're not quite——

[*He passes through the door into the house.* FER-RAND *stands at the fire, with his limbs spread as it were to embrace it, smoking with abandonment.* WELLWYN *returns stealthily, dressed in a Jaeger dressing-gown, and bearing a pair of drawers, his trousers, a pair of slippers, and a sweater.*

WELLWYN. [*Speaking in a low voice, for the door is still open.*] Can you make these do for the moment?

FERRAND. *Je vous remercie, Monsieur.* [*Pointing to the screen.*] May I retire?

WELLWYN. Yes, yes.

[FERRAND *goes behind the screen.* WELLWYN *closes the door into the house, then goes to the window to draw the curtains. He suddenly recoils and stands petrified with doubt.*

WELLWYN. Good Lord!

[*There is the sound of tapping on glass. Against the window-pane is pressed the face of a man.* WELLWYN *motions to him to go away. He does not go, but continues tapping.* WELLWYN *opens the door. There enters a square old man, with a red, pendulous-jawed, shaking face under a snow besprinkled bowler hat. He is holding out a visiting card with tremulous hand.*

WELLWYN. Who's that? Who are you?

TIMSON. [*In a thick, hoarse, shaking voice.*] 'Appy to see you, sir; we 'ad a talk this morning. Timson—I give you me name. You invited of me, if ye remember.

WELLWYN. It's a little late, really.

TIMSON. Well, ye see, I never expected to 'ave to call on yer. I was 'itched up all right when I spoke to yer this mornin', but bein' Christmas, things 'ave took a turn with me to-day. [*He speaks with increasing thickness.*] I'm reg'lar disgusted—not got the price of a bed abaht me. Thought you wouldn't like me to be delicate—not at my age.

WELLWYN. [*With a mechanical and distracted dive of his hands into his pockets.*] The fact is, it so happens I haven't a copper on me.

TIMSON. [*Evidently taking this for professional refusal.*] Wouldn't arsk you if I could 'elp it. 'Ad to do with 'orses all me life. It's this 'ere cold I'm frightened of. I'm afraid I'll go to sleep.

WELLWYN. Well, really, I——

TIMSON. To be froze to death—I mean—it's awkward.

WELLWYN. [*Puzzled and unhappy.*] Well—come in a moment, and let's—think it out. Have some tea!

> [*He pours out the remains of the tea, and finding there is not very much, adds rum rather liberally. TIMSON, who walks a little wide at the knees, steadying his gait, has followed.*]

TIMSON. [*Receiving the drink.*] Yer 'ealth. 'Ere's— soberiety! [*He applies the drink to his lips with shaking hand. Agreeably surprised.*] Blimey! Thish yer tea's foreign, ain't it?

FERRAND. [*Reappearing from behind the screen in his new clothes of which the trousers stop too soon.*] With a needle, Monsieur, I would soon have with what to make face against the world.

WELLWYN. Too short! Ah!

> [*He goes to the dais on which stands ANN's workbasket, and takes from it a needle and cotton.*
> [*While he is so engaged FERRAND is sizing up old TIMSON, as one dog will another. The old man, glass in hand, seems to have lapsed into coma.*]

FERRAND. [*Indicating* TIMSON.] Monsieur!

> [*He makes the gesture of one drinking, and shakes his head.*

WELLWYN. [*Handing him the needle and cotton.*] Um! Afraid so!

> [*They approach* TIMSON, *who takes no notice.*

FERRAND. [*Gently.*] It is an old cabby, is it not, Monsieur? *Ceux sont tous des buveurs.*

WELLWYN. [*Concerned at the old man's stupefaction.*] Now, my old friend, sit down a moment. [*They manœuvre* TIMSON *to the settle.*] Will you smoke?

TIMSON. [*In a drowsy voice.*] Thank 'ee—smoke pipe of 'baccer. Old 'orse—standin' abaht in th' cold.

> [*He relapses into coma.*

FERRAND. [*With a click of his tongue.*] *Il est parti.*

WELLWYN. [*Doubtfully.*] He hasn't really left a horse outside, do you think?

FERRAND. *Non, non, Monsieur*—no 'orse. He is dreaming. I know very well that state of him—that catches you sometimes. It is the warmth sudden on the stomach. He will speak no more sense to-night. At the most, drink, and fly a little in his past.

WELLWYN. Poor old buffer!

FERRAND. Touching, is it not, Monsieur? There are many brave gents among the old cabbies—they have philosophy—that comes from 'orses, and from sitting still.

WELLWYN. [*Touching* TIMSON's *shoulder.*] Drenched!

FERRAND. That will do 'im no 'arm, Monsieur—no 'arm at all. He is well wet inside, remember—it is

Christmas to-morrow. Put him a rug, if you will, he
will soon steam.

   [WELLWYN *takes up* ANN'S *long red cloak, and
    wraps it round the old man.*

 TIMSON. [*Faintly roused.*] Tha's right. Put—the
rug on th' old 'orse.

   [*He makes a strange noise, and works his head and
    tongue.*

 WELLWYN. [*Alarmed.*] What's the matter with him?

 FERRAND. It is nothing, Monsieur; for the moment
he thinks 'imself a 'orse. *Il joue* "*cache-cache*," 'ide
and seek, with what you call—'is bitt.

 WELLWYN. But what's to be done with him? One
can't turn him out in this state.

 FERRAND. If you wish to leave him 'ere, Monsieur,
have no fear. I charge myself with him.

 WELLWYN. Oh! [*Dubiously.*] You—er—I really don't
know, I—hadn't contemplated—You think you could
manage if I—if I went to bed?

 FERRAND. But certainly, Monsieur.

 WELLWYN. [*Still dubiously.*] You—you're sure you've
everything you want?

 FERRAND. [*Bowing.*] *Mais oui, Monsieur.*

 WELLWYN. I don't know what I can do by staying.

 FERRAND. There is nothing you can do, Monsieur.
Have confidence in me.

 WELLWYN. Well—keep the fire up quietly—very
quietly. You'd better take this coat of mine, too.
You'll find it precious cold, I expect, about three
o'clock.   [*He hands* FERRAND *his ulster.*

FERRAND. [*Taking it.*] I shall sleep in praying for you, Monsieur.

WELLWYN. Ah! Yes! Thanks! Well—good-night! By the way, I shall be down rather early. Have to think of my household a bit, you know.

FERRAND. *Très bien, Monsieur.* I comprehend. One must well be regular in this life.

WELLWYN. [*With a start.*] Lord! [*He looks at the door of the model's room.*] I'd forgotten——

FERRAND. Can I undertake anything, Monsieur?

WELLWYN. No, no! [*He goes to the electric light switch by the outer door.*] You won't want this, will you?

FERRAND. *Merci, Monsieur.*

[WELLWYN *switches off the light.*

FERRAND. *Bon soir, Monsieur!*

WELLWYN. The devil! Er—good-night!

[*He hesitates, rumples his hair, and passes rather suddenly away.*

FERRAND. [*To himself.*] Poor pigeon! [*Looking long at old* TIMSON.] *Espèce de type anglais!*

[*He sits down in the firelight, curls up a foot on his knee, and taking out a knife, rips the stitching of a turned-up end of trouser, pinches the cloth double, and puts in the preliminary stitch of a new hem—all with the swiftness of one well-accustomed. Then, as if hearing a sound behind him, he gets up quickly and slips behind the screen.* MRS. MEGAN, *attracted by the cessation of voices, has opened the door, and is creeping from the model's room towards the fire. She has*

*almost reached it before she takes in the torpid
crimson figure of old* TIMSON. *She halts and
puts her hand to her chest—a queer figure in the
firelight, garbed in the canary-coloured bath
gown and rabbit's-wool slippers, her black matted
hair straggling down on her neck. Having quite
digested the fact that the old man is in a sort of
stupor,* MRS. MEGAN *goes close to the fire, and
sits on the little stool, smiling sideways at old*
TIMSON. FERRAND, *coming quietly up behind,
examines her from above, drooping his long nose
as if enquiring with it as to her condition in
life; then he steps back a yard or two.*

FERRAND. [*Gently.*] Pardon, Ma'moiselle.

MRS. MEGAN. [*Springing to her feet.*] Oh!

FERRAND. All right, all right! We are brave gents!

TIMSON. [*Faintly roused.*] 'Old up, there!

FERRAND. Trust in me, Ma'moiselle!

          [MRS. MEGAN *responds by drawing away.*

FERRAND. [*Gently.*] We must be good comrades.
This asylum—it is better than a doss-'ouse.

          [*He pushes the stool over towards her, and seats
          himself. Somewhat reassured,* MRS. MEGAN
          again sits down.

MRS. MEGAN. You frightened me.

TIMSON. [*Unexpectedly—in a drowsy tone.*] Purple
foreigners!

FERRAND. Pay no attention, Ma'moiselle. He is a
philosopher.

MRS. MEGAN. Oh! I thought 'e was boozed.

> [*They both look at* TIMSON.

FERRAND. It is the same—veree 'armless.

MRS. MEGAN. What's that he's got on 'im?

FERRAND. It is a coronation robe. Have no fear, Ma'moiselle. Veree docile potentate.

MRS. MEGAN. I wouldn't be afraid of him. [*Challenging* FERRAND.] I'm afraid o' *you*.

FERRAND. It is because you do not know me, Ma'moiselle. You are wrong, it is always the unknown you should love.

MRS. MEGAN. I don't like the way you—speaks to me.

FERRAND. Ah! You are a Princess in disguise?

MRS. MEGAN. No fear!

FERRAND. No? What is it then you do to make face against the necessities of life? A living?

MRS. MEGAN. Sells flowers.

FERRAND. [*Rolling his eyes.*] It is not a career.

MRS. MEGAN. [*With a touch of devilry.*] You don't know what I do.

FERRAND. Ma'moiselle, whatever you do is charming.

> [MRS. MEGAN *looks at him, and slowly smiles.*

MRS. MEGAN. You're a foreigner.

FERRAND. It is true.

MRS. MEGAN. What do *you* do for a livin'?

FERRAND. I am an interpreter.

MRS. MEGAN. You ain't very busy, are you?

FERRAND. [*With dignity.*] At present I am resting.

MRS. MEGAN. [*Looking at him and smiling.*] How did you and 'im come here?

FERRAND. Ma'moiselle, we would ask you the same question.

MRS. MEGAN. The gentleman let me. 'E's funny.

FERRAND. *C'est un ange!* [*At* MRS. MEGAN's *blank stare he interprets.*] An angel!

MRS. MEGAN. Me luck's out—that's why I come.

FERRAND. [*Rising.*] Ah! Ma'moiselle! Luck! There is the little God who dominates us all. Look at this old! [*He points to* TIMSON.] He is finished. In his day that old would be doing good business. He could afford himself— [*He makes a sign of drinking.*] Then come the motor cars. All goes—he has nothing left, only 'is 'abits of a cocher! Luck!

TIMSON. [*With a vague gesture—drowsily.*] Kick the foreign beggars out.

FERRAND. A real Englishman. . . . And look at me! My father was merchant of ostrich feathers in Brussels. If I had been content to go in his business, I would 'ave been rich. But I was born to roll—"rolling stone"— to voyage is stronger than myself. Luck! . . . And you, Ma'moiselle, shall I tell your fortune? [*He looks in her face.*] You were born for *la joie de vivre*—to drink the wines of life. *Et vous voilà!* Luck!

> [*Though she does not in the least understand what he has said, her expression changes to a sort of glee.*

FERRAND. Yes. You were born loving pleasure. Is it not? You see, you cannot say, No. All of us, we have our fates. Give me your hand. [*He kneels down and takes her hand.*] In each of us there is that against which we cannot struggle.   Yes, yes!

> [*He holds her hand, and turns it over between his own.   Mrs. Megan remains stolid, half-fascinated, half-reluctant.*

Timson. [*Flickering into consciousness.*] Be'ave yourselves!   Yer crimson canary birds!

> [Mrs. Megan *would withdraw her hand, but cannot.*

Ferrand. Pay no attention, Ma'moiselle.   He is a Puritan.

> [Timson *relapses into comatosity, upsetting his glass, which falls with a crash.*

Mrs. Megan. Let go my hand, please!

Ferrand. [*Relinquishing it, and staring into the fire gravely.*] There is one thing I have never done—'urt a woman—that is hardly in my character. [*Then, drawing a little closer, he looks into her face.*] Tell me, Ma'moiselle, what is it you think of all day long?

Mrs. Megan. I dunno—lots, I thinks of.

Ferrand. Shall I tell you? [*Her eyes remain fixed on his, the strangeness of him preventing her from telling him to "get along."   He goes on in his ironic voice.*] It is of the streets—the lights—the faces—it is of all which moves, and is warm—it is of colour—it is [*he brings his face quite close to hers*] of Love.   That is for you what the road is for me.   That is for you what the rum is for that old— [*He jerks his thumb back at* Timson.   *Then bending swiftly forward to the girl.*] See!   I kiss you—Ah!

> [*He draws her forward off the stool.   There is a little struggle, then she resigns her lips.   The*

little stool, overturned, falls with a clatter. They spring up, and move apart. The door opens and ANN *enters from the house in a blue dressing-gown, with her hair loose, and a candle held high above her head. Taking in the strange half-circle round the stove, she recoils. Then, standing her ground, calls in a voice sharpened by fright:* "Daddy—Daddy!"

TIMSON. [*Stirring uneasily, and struggling to his feet.*] All ri——! I'm comin'!

FERRAND. Have no fear, Madame!

[*In the silence that follows, a clock begins loudly striking twelve.* ANN *remains, as if carved in stone, her eyes fastened on the strangers. There is the sound of someone falling downstairs, and* WELLWYN *appears, also holding a candle above his head.*

ANN. Look!

WELLWYN. Yes, yes, my dear! It—it happened.

ANN. [*With a sort of groan.*] Oh! Daddy!

[*In the renewed silence, the church clock ceases to chime.*

FERRAND. [*Softly, in his ironic voice.*] HE is come, Monsieur! 'Appy Christmas! Bon Noël!

[*There is a sudden chime of bells. The Stage is blotted dark.*

Curtain.

ACT II

It is four o'clock in the afternoon of New Year's Day.
On the raised dais MRS. MEGAN *is standing, in her*
rags; with bare feet and ankles, her dark hair as if
blown about, her lips parted, holding out a dishevelled
bunch of violets. Before his easel, WELLWYN *is*
painting her. Behind him, at a table between the
cupboard and the door to the model's room, TIMSON *is*
washing brushes, with the movements of one employed
upon relief works. The samovar is hissing on the
table by the stove, the tea things are set out.

WELLWYN. Open your mouth.

> [MRS. MEGAN *opens her mouth.*

ANN. [*In hat and coat, entering from the house.*]
Daddy!

> [WELLWYN *goes to her; and, released from re-*
> *straint,* MRS. MEGAN *looks round at* TIMSON
> *and grimaces.*

WELLWYN. Well, my dear?

> [*They speak in low voices.*

ANN. [*Holding out a note.*] This note from Canon
Bertley. He's going to bring her husband here this
afternoon.   [*She looks at* MRS. MEGAN.

WELLWYN. Oh!   [*He also looks at* MRS. MEGAN.

27

ANN. And I met Sir Thomas Hoxton at church this morning, and spoke to him about Timson.

WELLWYN. Um!

> [*They look at* TIMSON. *Then* ANN *goes back to the door, and* WELLWYN *follows her.*

ANN. [*Turning.*] I'm going round now, Daddy, to ask Professor Calway what we're to do with that Ferrand.

WELLWYN. Oh! One each! I wonder if they'll like it.

ANN. They'll have to lump it.

> [*She goes out into the house.*

WELLWYN. [*Back at his easel.*] You can shut your mouth now.

> [MRS. MEGAN *shuts her mouth, but opens it immediately to smile.*

WELLWYN. [*Spasmodically.*] Ah! Now that's what I want. [*He dabs furiously at the canvas. Then standing back, runs his hands through his hair and turns a painter's glance towards the skylight.*] Dash! Light's gone! Off you get, child—don't tempt me!

> [MRS. MEGAN *descends. Passing towards the door of the model's room she stops, and stealthily looks at the picture.*

TIMSON. Ah! Would yer!

WELLWYN. [*Wheeling round.*] Want to have a look? Well—come on!

> [*He takes her by the arm, and they stand before the canvas. After a stolid moment, she giggles.*

WELLWYN. Oh! You think so?

MRS. MEGAN. [*Who has lost her hoarseness.*] It's not like my picture that I had on the pier.

WELLWYN. No—it wouldn't be.

MRS. MEGAN. [*Timidly.*] If I had an 'at on, I'd look better.

WELLWYN. With feathers?

MRS. MEGAN. Yes.

WELLWYN. Well, you can't! I don't like hats, and I don't like feathers.

[MRS. MEGAN *timidly tugs his sleeve.* TIMSON, *screened as he thinks by the picture, has drawn from his bulky pocket a bottle and is taking a stealthy swig.*

WELLWYN. [*To* MRS. MEGAN, *affecting not to notice.*] How much do I owe you?

MRS. MEGAN. [*A little surprised.*] You paid me for to-day—all 'cept a penny.

WELLWYN. Well! Here it is. [*He gives her a coin.*] Go and get your feet on!

MRS. MEGAN. You've give me 'arf a crown.

WELLWYN. Cut away now!

[MRS. MEGAN, *smiling at the coin, goes towards the model's room. She looks back at* WELLWYN, *as if to draw his eyes to her, but he is gazing at the picture; then, catching old* TIMSON'S *sour glance, she grimaces at him, kicking up her feet with a little squeal. But when* WELLWYN *turns to the sound, she is demurely passing through the doorway.*

TIMSON. [*In his voice of dubious sobriety.*] I've finished these yer brushes, sir. It's not a man's work.
I've been thinkin' if you'd keep an 'orse, I could give
yer satisfaction.

WELLWYN. Would the horse, Timson?

TIMSON. [*Looking him up and down.*] I knows of one
that would just suit yer. Reel 'orse, you'd like 'im.

WELLWYN. [*Shaking his head.*] Afraid not, Timson!
Awfully sorry, though, to have nothing better for you
than this, at present.

TIMSON. [*Faintly waving the brushes.*] Of course, if
you can't afford it, I don't press you—it's only that. I
feel I'm not doing meself justice. [*Confidentially.*]
There's just one thing, sir; I can't bear to see a gen'leman imposed on. That foreigner—'e's not the sort to
'ave about the place. Talk? Oh! ah! But 'e'll never
do any good with 'imself. He's a alien.

WELLWYN. Terrible misfortune to a fellow, Timson.

TIMSON. Don't you believe it, sir; it's his *fault* I
says to the young lady yesterday: Miss Ann, your
father's a gen'leman [*with a sudden accent of hoarse sincerity*], and so you are—I don't mind sayin' it—*but*, I
said, he's too easy-goin'.

WELLWYN. Indeed!

TIMSON. Well, see that girl now! [*He shakes his head.*]
I never did believe in goin' behind a person's back—
I'm an Englishman—but [*lowering his voice*] she's a
bad hat, sir. Why, look at the street she comes from!

WELLWYN. Oh! you know it.

TIMSON. Lived there meself larst three years. See

the difference a few days' corn's made in her.   She's
that saucy you can't touch 'er head.

WELLWYN. Is there any necessity, Timson?

TIMSON. Artful too.   Full o' vice, I call 'er.   Where's
'er 'usband?

WELLWYN. [*Gravely.*] Come, Timson!   You wouldn't
like *her* to——

TIMSON. [*With dignity, so that the bottle in his pocket
is plainly visible.*] I'm a man as always beared inspec-
tion.

WELLWYN. [*With a well-directed smile.*] So I see.

TIMSON. [*Curving himself round the bottle.*] It's not
for me to say nothing—but I can tell a gen'leman as
quick as ever I can tell an 'orse.

WELLWYN. [*Painting.*] I find it safest to assume
that every man is a gentleman, and every woman a
lady.   Saves no end of self-contempt.   Give me the
little brush.

TIMSON. [*Handing him the brush—after a consider-
able introspective pause.*] Would yer like me to stay and
wash it for yer again? [*With great resolution.*] I will—
I'll do it for you—never grudged workin' for a gen'leman.

WELLWYN. [*With sincerity.*] Thank you, Timson—
very good of you, I'm sure. [*He hands him back the
brush.*] Just lend us a hand with this. [*Assisted by* TIM-
SON *he pushes back the dais.*] Let's see!   What do I owe
you?

TIMSON. [*Reluctantly.*] It so 'appens, you advanced
me to-day's yesterday.

WELLWYN. Then I suppose you want to-morrow's?

TIMSON. Well, I 'ad to spend it, lookin' for a permanent job. When you've got to do with 'orses, you can't neglect the publics, or you might as well be dead.

WELLWYN. Quite so!

TIMSON. It mounts up in the course o' the year.

WELLWYN. It would. [*Passing him a coin.*] This is for an exceptional purpose—Timson—see. Not——

TIMSON. [*Touching his forehead.*] Certainly, sir. I quite understand. I'm not that sort, as I think I've proved to yer, comin' here regular day after day, all the week. There's one thing, I ought to warn you perhaps—I might 'ave to give this job up any day.

> [*He makes a faint demonstration with the little brush, then puts it, absent-mindedly, into his pocket.*

WELLWYN. [*Gravely.*] I'd never stand in the way of your bettering yourself, Timson. And, by the way, my daughter spoke to a friend about you to-day. I think something may come of it.

TIMSON. Oh! Oh! She did! Well, it might do me a bit o' good. [*He makes for the outer door, but stops.*] That foreigner! 'E sticks in my gizzard. It's not as if there wasn't plenty o' pigeons for 'im to pluck in 'is own Gawd-forsaken country. Reg-lar jay, that's what I calls 'im. I could tell yer something——

> [*He has opened the door, and suddenly sees that FERRAND himself is standing there. Sticking out his lower lip, TIMSON gives a roll of his jaw*

and lurches forth into the street. Owing to a
slight miscalculation, his face and raised arms
are plainly visible through the window, as he for-
tifies himself from his battle against the cold.
FERRAND, *having closed the door, stands with*
his thumb acting as pointer towards this spectacle.
He is now remarkably dressed in an artist's
squashy green hat, a frock coat too small for him,
a bright blue tie of knitted silk, the grey trousers
that were torn, well-worn brown boots, and a tan
waistcoat.

WELLWYN. What luck to-day?

FERRAND. [*With a shrug.*] Again I have beaten all
London, Monsieur—not one bite. [*Contemplating himself.*] I think perhaps, that, for the bourgeoisie, there is
a little too much colour in my costume.

WELLWYN. [*Contemplating him.*] Let's see—I believe I've an old top hat somewhere.

FERRAND. Ah! Monsieur, *merci,* but *that* I could
not. It is scarcely in my character.

WELLWYN. True!

FERRAND. I have been to merchants of wine, of *tabac,*
to hotels, to Leicester Square. I have been to a—
Society for spreading Christian knowledge—I thought
there I would have a chance perhaps as interpreter.
Toujours même chose—we regret, we have no situation
for you—same thing everywhere. It seems there is
nothing doing in this town.

WELLWYN. I've noticed, there never is.

FERRAND. I was thinking, Monsieur, that in **avia-**

tion there might be a career for me—but it seems one must be trained.

WELLWYN. Afraid so, Ferrand.

FERRAND. [*Approaching the picture.*] Ah! You are always working at this. You will have something of very good there, Monsieur. You wish to fix the type of wild savage existing ever amongst our high civilisation. *C'est très chic ça!* [WELLWYN *manifests the quiet delight of an English artist actually understood.*] In the figures of these good citizens, to whom she offers her flower, you would give the idea of all the cage doors open to catch and make tame the wild bird, that will surely die within. *Très gentil!* Believe me, Monsieur, you have there the greatest comedy of life! How anxious are the tame birds to do the wild birds good. [*His voice changes.*] For the wild birds it is not funny. There is in some human souls, Monsieur, what cannot be made tame.

WELLWYN. I believe you, Ferrand.

> [*The face of a young man appears at the window, unseen. Suddenly* ANN *opens the door leading to the house.*]

ANN. Daddy—I want you.

WELLWYN. [*To* FERRAND.] Excuse me a minute!

> [*He goes to his daughter, and they pass out.*
> [FERRAND *remains at the picture.* MRS. MEGAN *dressed in some of* ANN'S *discarded garments, has come out of the model's room. She steals up behind* FERRAND *like a cat, reaches an arm up, and curls it round his mouth. He turns, and*

> *tries to seize her; she disingenuously slips away.*
> *He follows.   The chase circles the tea table.   He*
> *catches her, lifts her up, swings round with her,*
> *so that her feet fly out; kisses her bent-back face,*
> *and sets her down.   She stands there smiling.*
> *The face at the window darkens.*

FERRAND.   La Valse!

> [*He takes her with both hands by the waist, she puts*
> *her hands against his shoulders to push him off*
> *—and suddenly they are whirling.   As they*
> *whirl, they bob together once or twice, and kiss.*
> *Then, with a warning motion towards the door,*
> *she wrenches herself free, and stops beside the*
> *picture, trying desperately to appear demure.*
> WELLWYN *and* ANN *have entered.   The face*
> *has vanished.*

FERRAND. [*Pointing to the picture.*] One does not
comprehend all this, Monsieur, without well studying.
I was in train to interpret for Ma'moiselle the chiaro-
scuro.

WELLWYN. [*With a queer look.*] Don't take it *too*
seriously, Ferrand.

FERRAND.   It is a masterpiece.

WELLWYN.   My daughter's just spoken to a friend,
Professor Calway.   He'd like to meet you.   Could you
come back a little later?

FERRAND.   Certainly, Ma'moiselle.   That will be an
opening for me, I trust.   [*He goes to the street door.*

ANN. [*Paying no attention to him.*] Mrs. Megan, will
you too come back in half an hour?

FERRAND. *Très bien, Ma'moiselle!* I will see that she does. We will take a little promenade together. That will do us good.

> [*He motions towards the door;* MRS. MEGAN, *all eyes, follows him out.*

ANN. Oh! Daddy, they *are* rotters. Couldn't you *see* they were having the most high jinks?

WELLWYN. [*At his picture.*] I seemed to have noticed something.

ANN. [*Preparing for tea.*] They were kissing.

WELLWYN. Tt! Tt!

ANN. They're hopeless, all three—especially her. Wish I hadn't given her my clothes now.

WELLWYN. [*Absorbed.*] Something of wild-savage.

ANN. Thank goodness it's the Vicar's business to see that married people live together in his parish.

WELLWYN. Oh! [*Dubiously.*] The Megans are Roman Catholic-Atheists, Ann.

ANN. [*With heat.*] Then they're all the more bound.

> [WELLWYN *gives a sudden and alarmed whistle.*

ANN. What's the matter?

WELLWYN. Didn't you say you spoke to Sir Thomas, too. Suppose he comes in while the Professor's here. They're cat and dog.

ANN. [*Blankly.*] Oh! [*As* WELLWYN *strikes a match.*] The samovar *is* lighted. [*Taking up the nearly empty decanter of rum and going to the cupboard.*] It's all right. He won't.

WELLWYN. We'll hope not.

> [*He turns back to his picture.*

ANN. [*At the cupboard.*] Daddy!

WELLWYN. Hi!

ANN. There were *three bottles*.

WELLWYN. Oh!

ANN. Well! Now there aren't any.

WELLWYN. [*Abstracted.*] That'll be Timson.

ANN. [*With real horror.*] But it's awful!

WELLWYN. It is, my dear.

ANN. In seven days.   To say nothing of the stealing.

WELLWYN. [*Vexed.*] I blame myself—very much. Ought to have kept it locked up.

ANN. You ought to keep *him* locked up!

      [*There is heard a mild but authoritative knock.*

WELLWYN. Here's the Vicar!

ANN. What are you going to do about the rum?

WELLWYN. [*Opening the door to* CANON BERTLEY.] Come in, Vicar! Happy New Year!

BERTLEY. Same to you! Ah! Ann! I've got into touch with her young husband—he's coming round.

ANN. [*Still a little out of her plate.*] Thank Go—— Moses!

BERTLEY. [*Faintly surprised.*] From what I hear he's not really a bad youth.   Afraid he bets on horses.   The great thing, Wellwyn, with those poor fellows is to put your finger on the weak spot.

ANN. [*To herself—gloomily.*] That's not difficult. What would you do, Canon Bertley, with a man who's been drinking father's rum?

BERTLEY. Remove the temptation, of course.

WELLWYN. He's done that.

BERTLEY. Ah! Then— [WELLWYN *and* ANN *hang on his words*] then I should—er——

ANN. [*Abruptly.*] Remove *him.*

BERTLEY. Before I say that, Ann, I must certainly see the individual.

WELLWYN. [*Pointing to the window.*] There he is!
        [*In the failing light* TIMSON'S *face is indeed to be
            seen pressed against the window pane.*

ANN. Daddy, I do wish you'd have thick glass put in. It's so disgusting to be spied at! [WELLWYN *going quickly to the door, has opened it.*] What do you want?
                [TIMSON *enters with dignity. He is fuddled.*

TIMSON. [*Slowly.*] Arskin' yer pardon—thought it me duty to come back—found thish yer little brishel on me.   [*He produces the little paint brush.*

ANN. [*In a deadly voice.*] Nothing else?
                        [TIMSON *accords her a glassy stare.*

WELLWYN. [*Taking the brush hastily.*] That'll do, Timson, thanks!

TIMSON. As I am 'ere, can I do anything for yer?

ANN. Yes, you can sweep out that little room. [*She points to the model's room.*] There's a broom in there.

TIMSON. [*Disagreeably surprised.*] Certainly; never make bones about a little extra—never 'ave in all me life. Do it at onsh, I will. [*He moves across to the model's room at that peculiar broad gait so perfectly adjusted to his habits.*] You quite understand me—couldn't bear to 'ave anything on me that wasn't mine.

                                [*He passes out.*

ANN. Old fraud!

WELLWYN. "In" and "on." Mark my words, he'll restore the—bottles.

BERTLEY. But, my dear Wellwyn, that *is* stealing.

WELLWYN. We all have our discrepancies, Vicar.

ANN. Daddy! Discrepancies!

WELLWYN. Well, Ann, my theory is that as regards solids Timson's an Individualist, but as regards liquids he's a Socialist . . . or *vice versâ*, according to taste.

BERTLEY. No, no, we mustn't joke about it. [*Gravely.*] I do think he should be spoken to.

WELLWYN. Yes, but not by me.

BERTLEY. Surely you're the proper person.

WELLWYN. [*Shaking his head.*] It was my rum, Vicar. Look so personal.

> [*There sound a number of little tat-tat knocks.*

WELLWYN. Isn't that the Professor's knock?

> [*While Ann sits down to make tea, he goes to the door and opens it. There, dressed in an ulster, stands a thin, clean-shaved man, with a little hollow sucked into either cheek, who, taking off a grey squash hat, discloses a majestically bald forehead, which completely dominates all that comes below it.*

WELLWYN. Come in, Professor! So awfully good of you! You know Canon Bertley, I think?

CALWAY. Ah! How d'you do?

WELLWYN. Your opinion will be invaluable, Professor.

ANN. Tea, Professor Calway?

> [*They have assembled round the tea table.*

CALWAY. Thank you; no tea; milk.

WELLWYN. Rum?

[*He pours rum into* CALWAY's *milk.*

CALWAY. A little—thanks! [*Turning to* ANN.] You were going to show me some one you're trying to rescue, or something, I think.

ANN. Oh! Yes. He'll be here directly—simply perfect rotter.

CALWAY. [*Smiling.*] Really! Ah! I think you said he was a congenital?

WELLWYN. [*With great interest.*] What!

ANN. [*Low.*] Daddy! [*To* CALWAY.] Yes; I—I think that's what you call him.

CALWAY. Not old?

ANN. No; and quite healthy—a vagabond.

CALWAY. [*Sipping.*] I see! Yes. Is it, do you think chronic unemployment with a vagrant tendency? Or would it be nearer the mark to say: Vagrancy——

WELLWYN. Pure! Oh! pure! Professor. Awfully human.

CALWAY. [*With a smile of knowledge.*] Quite! And —er——

ANN. [*Breaking in.*] Before he comes, there's another——

BERTLEY. [*Blandly.*] Yes, when you came in, we were discussing what should be done with a man who drinks rum— [CALWAY *pauses in the act of drinking*] that doesn't belong to him.

CALWAY. Really! Dipsomaniac?

BERTLEY. Well—perhaps you could tell us—drink

certainly changing thine to mine. The Professor could see him, Wellwyn?

ANN. [*Rising.*] Yes, do come and look at him, Professor Calway. He's in there.

[*She points towards the model's room.* CALWAY *smiles deprecatingly.*

ANN. No, *really;* we needn't open the door. You can see him through the glass. He's more than half——

CALWAY. Well, I hardly——

ANN. Oh! Do! Come on, Professor Calway! We *must* know what to do with him. [CALWAY *rises.*] You can stand on a chair. It's all science.

[*She draws* CALWAY *to the model's room, which is lighted by a glass panel in the top of the high door.* CANON BERTLEY *also rises and stands watching.* WELLWYN *hovers, torn between respect for science and dislike of espionage.*

ANN. [*Drawing up a chair.*] Come on!

CALWAY. Do you seriously wish me to?

ANN. Rather! It's quite safe; he can't see you.

CALWAY. But he might come out.

[ANN *puts her back against the door.* CALWAY *mounts the chair dubiously, and raises his head cautiously, bending it more and more downwards.*

ANN. Well?

CALWAY. He appears to be—sitting on the floor.

WELLWYN. Yes, that's all right!

[BERTLEY *covers his lips.*

CALWAY. [*To* ANN—*descending.*] By the look of his

face, as far as one can see it, I should say there was a leaning towards mania.   I know the treatment.

> [*There come three loud knocks on the door.* WELL-
> WYN *and* ANN *exchange a glance of consterna-
> tion.*

ANN. Who's that?

WELLWYN. It sounds like Sir Thomas.

CALWAY. Sir Thomas Hoxton?

WELLWYN. [*Nodding.*] Awfully sorry, Professor. You see, we——

CALWAY. Not at all.   Only, I must decline to be involved in argument with him, please.

BERTLEY. He has experience.   We might get his opinion, don't you think?

CALWAY. On a point of reform?   A J.P.!

BERTLEY. [*Deprecating.*] My dear Sir—we needn't take it.

> [*The three knocks resound with extraordinary fury.*

ANN. You'd better open the door, Daddy.

> [WELLWYN *opens the door.* SIR THOMAS HOX-
> TON *is disclosed in a fur overcoat and top hat.
> His square, well-coloured face is remarkable for
> a massive jaw, dominating all that comes above
> it.   His voice is resolute.*

HOXTON. Afraid I didn't make myself heard.

WELLWYN. So good of you to come, Sir Thomas. Canon Bertley! [*They greet.*] Professor Calway you know, I think.

HOXTON. [*Ominously.*] I do.

> [*They almost greet.   An awkward pause.*

ANN. [*Blurting it out.*] That old cabman I told you of's been drinking father's rum.

BERTLEY. We were just discussing what's to be done with him, Sir Thomas. One wants to do the very best, of course. The question of reform is always delicate.

CALWAY. I beg your pardon. There *is* no question here.

HOXTON. [*Abruptly.*] Oh! Is he in the house?

ANN. In there.

HOXTON. Works for you, eh?

WELLWYN. Er—yes.

HOXTON. Let's have a look at him!

[*An embarrassed pause.*

BERTLEY. Well—the fact is, Sir Thomas——

CALWAY. When last under observation——

ANN. He was sitting on the floor.

WELLWYN. I don't want the old fellow to feel he's being made a show of. Disgusting to be spied at, Ann.

ANN. You can't, Daddy! He's drunk.

HOXTON. Never mind, Miss Wellwyn. Hundreds of these fellows before me in my time. [*At* CALWAY.] The only thing is a sharp lesson!

CALWAY. I disagree. I've seen the man; what he requires is steady control, and the Dobbins treatment.

[WELLWYN *approaches them with fearful interest.*

HOXTON. Not a bit of it! He wants one for his knob! Brace 'em up! It's the only thing.

BERTLEY. Personally, I think that if he were spoken to seriously——

CALWAY. I cannot walk arm in arm with a crab!

Hoxton. [*Approaching* Calway.] I beg your pardon?

Calway. [*Moving back a little.*] You're moving backwards, Sir Thomas. I've told you before, convinced reactionaryism, in these days——

    [*There comes a single knock on the street door.*

Bertley. [*Looking at his watch.*] D'you know, I'm rather afraid this may be our young husband, Wellwyn. I told him half-past four.

Wellwyn. Oh! Ah! Yes. [*Going towards the two reformers.*] Shall we go into the house, Professor, and settle the question quietly while the Vicar sees a young man?

Calway. [*Pale with uncompleted statement, and gravitating insensibly in the direction indicated.*] The merest sense of continuity—a simple instinct for order——

Hoxton. [*Following.*] The only way to get order, sir, is to bring the disorderly up with a round turn. [Calway *turns to him in the doorway.*] You people without practical experience——

Calway. If you'll listen to me a minute.

Hoxton. I can show you in a mo——

    [*They vanish through the door.*

Wellwyn. I was afraid of it.

Bertley. The two points of view. Pleasant to see such keenness. I may want you, Wellwyn. And Ann perhaps had better not be present.

Wellwyn. [*Relieved.*] Quite so! My dear!

    [Ann *goes reluctantly.* Wellwyn *opens the*
    street door. The lamp outside has just been
    lighted, and, by its gleam, is seen the figure of

RORY MEGAN, *thin, pale, youthful.* ANN *turning at the door into the house gives him a long, inquisitive look, then goes.*

WELLWYN. Is that Megan?

MEGAN. Yus.

WELLWYN. Come in.

[MEGAN *comes in. There follows an awkward silence, during which* WELLWYN *turns up the light, then goes to the tea table and pours out a glass of tea and rum.*

BERTLEY. [*Kindly.*] Now, my boy, how is it that you and your wife are living apart like this?

MEGAN. I dunno.

BERTLEY. Well, if *you* don't, none of us are very likely to, are we?

MEGAN. That's what I thought, as I was comin' along.

WELLWYN. [*Twinkling.*] Have some tea, Megan? [*Handing him the glass.*] What d'you think of her picture? 'Tisn't quite finished.

MEGAN. [*After scrutiny.*] I seen her look like it—once.

WELLWYN. Good! When was that?

MEGAN. [*Stoically.*] When she 'ad the measles.

[*He drinks.*

WELLWYN. [*Ruminating.*] I see—yes. I quite see— feverish!

BERTLEY. My dear Wellwyn, let me—— [*To* MEGAN.] Now, I hope you're willing to come together again, and to maintain her?

MEGAN. If she'll maintain me.

BERTLEY. Oh! but—— I see, you mean you're in the same line of business?

MEGAN. Yus.

BERTLEY. And lean on each other.   Quite so!

MEGAN. I leans on 'er mostly—with 'er looks.

BERTLEY. Indeed!   Very interesting—that!

MEGAN. Yus.   Sometimes she'll take 'arf a crown off of a toff.   [*He looks at* WELLWYN.

WELLWYN. [*Twinkling.*] I apologise to you, Megan.

MEGAN. [*With a faint smile.*] I could do with a bit more of it.

BERTLEY. [*Dubiously.*] Yes! Yes! Now, my boy, I've heard you bet on horses.

MEGAN. No, I don't.

BERTLEY. Play cards, then? Come! Don't be afraid to acknowledge it.

MEGAN. When I'm 'ard up—yus.

BERTLEY. But don't you know that's ruination?

MEGAN. Depends.   Sometimes I wins a lot.

BERTLEY. You know that's not at all what I mean. Come, promise me to give it up.

MEGAN. I dunno abaht that.

BERTLEY. Now, there's a good fellow.   Make a big effort and throw the habit off!

MEGAN. Comes over me—same as it might over you.

BERTLEY. Over me!   How do you mean, my boy?

MEGAN. [*With a look up.*] To tork!

      [WELLWYN, *turning to the picture, makes a funny
         little noise.*

BERTLEY. [*Maintaining his good humour.*] A hit! But you forget, you know, to talk's my business. It's not yours to gamble.

MEGAN. You try sellin' flowers. If that ain't a— gamble——

BERTLEY. I'm afraid we're wandering a little from the point. Husband and wife should be together. You were brought up to that. Your father and mother——

MEGAN. Never was.

WELLWYN. [*Turning from the picture.*] The question is, Megan: Will you take your wife home? She's a good little soul.

MEGAN. She never let me know it.

[*There is a feeble knock on the door.*

WELLWYN. Well, now come. Here she is!

[*He points to the door, and stands regarding MEGAN with his friendly smile.*

MEGAN. [*With a gleam of responsiveness.*] I might, perhaps, to please *you*, sir.

BERTLEY. [*Appropriating the gesture.*] Capital, I thought we should get on in time.

MEGAN. Yus.

[WELLWYN *opens the door.* MRS. MEGAN *and* FERRAND *are revealed. They are about to enter, but catching sight of* MEGAN, *hesitate.*

BERTLEY. Come in! Come in!

[MRS. MEGAN *enters stolidly.* FERRAND, *following, stands apart with an air of extreme detachment.* MEGAN, *after a quick glance at them*

*both, remains unmoved. No one has noticed
that the door of the model's room has been opened,
and that the unsteady figure of old* TIMSON *is
standing there.*

BERTLEY. [*A little awkward in the presence of* FER-
RAND—*to the* MEGANS.] This begins a new chapter.
We won't improve the occasion. No need.

    [MEGAN, *turning towards his wife, makes her a
    gesture as if to say:* "Here! let's get out of
    this!"]

BERTLEY. Yes, yes, you'll like to get home at once
—I know.   [*He holds up his hand mechanically.*

TIMSON. I forbids the banns.

BERTLEY. [*Startled.*] Gracious!

TIMSON. [*Extremely unsteady.*] Just cause and im-
pejiment. There 'e stands. [*He points to* FERRAND.]
The crimson foreigner! The mockin' jay!

WELLWYN. Timson!

TIMSON. You're a gen'leman—I'm aweer o' that—
but I must speak the truth—[*he waves his hand*] an'
shame the devil!

BERTLEY. Is this the rum——?

TIMSON. [*Struck by the word.*] I'm a teetotaler.

WELLWYN. Timson, Timson!

TIMSON. Seein' as there's ladies present, I won't be
conspicuous. [*Moving away, and making for the door,
he strikes against the dais, and mounts upon it.*] But what
I do say, is: He's no better than 'er and she's worse.

BERTLEY. This is distressing.

FERRAND. [*Calmly.*] On my honour, Monsieur!

[TIMSON *growls.*

WELLWYN. Now, now, Timson!

TIMSON. That's all right. You're a gen'leman, an' I'm a gen'leman, but he ain't an' she ain't.

WELLWYN. We shall not believe you.

BERTLEY. No, no; we shall not believe you.

TIMSON. [*Heavily.*] Very well, you doubts my word. Will it make any difference, Guv'nor, if I speaks the truth?

BERTLEY. No, certainly not—that is—of course, it will.

TIMSON. Well, then, I see 'em plainer than I see [*pointing at* BERTLEY] the two of you.

WELLWYN. Be quiet, Timson!

BERTLEY. Not even her husband believes you.

MEGAN. [*Suddenly.*] Don't I!

WELLWYN. Come, Megan, you can see the old fellow's in Paradise.

BERTLEY. Do you credit such a—such an object?

[*He points at* TIMSON, *who seems falling asleep.*

MEGAN. Naow!

[*Unseen by anybody,* ANN *has returned.*

BERTLEY. Well, then, my boy?

MEGAN. I seen 'em meself.

BERTLEY. Gracious! But just now you were willing——

MEGAN. [*Sardonically.*] There wasn't nothing against me honour, then. Now you've took it away between you, comin' aht with it like this. I don't want no more

of 'er, and I'll want a good deal more of 'im; as 'e'll
soon find.

> [*He jerks his chin at* FERRAND, *turns slowly on
> his heel, and goes out into the street.*
>
> > [*There follows a profound silence.*

ANN. What did I say, Daddy? Utter! All three.

> [*Suddenly alive to her presence, they all turn.*

TIMSON. [*Waking up and looking round him.*] Well,
p'raps I'd better go.

> [*Assisted by* WELLWYN *he lurches gingerly off the
> dais towards the door, which* WELLWYN *holds
> open for him.*

TIMSON. [*Mechanically.*] Where to, sir?

> [*Receiving no answer he passes out, touching his
> hat; and the door is closed.*

WELLWYN. Ann!

> [ANN *goes back whence she came.*
>
> [BERTLEY, *steadily regarding* MRS. MEGAN, *who
> has put her arm up in front of her face, beckons
> to* FERRAND, *and the young man comes gravely
> forward.*

BERTLEY. Young people, this is very dreadful.
[MRS. MEGAN *lowers her arm a little, and looks at him
over it.*] Very sad!

MRS. MEGAN. [*Dropping her arm.*] Megan's no better than what I am.

BERTLEY. Come, come! Here's your home broken
up! [MRS. MEGAN *smiles. Shaking his head gravely.*]
Surely—surely—you mustn't smile. [MRS. MEGAN *be-
comes tragic.*] That's better. Now, what is to be done?

FERRAND. Believe me, Monsieur, I greatly regret.

BERTLEY. I'm glad to hear it.

FERRAND. If I had foreseen this disaster.

BERTLEY. Is that your only reason for regret?

FERRAND. [*With a little bow.*] Any reason that you wish, Monsieur. I will do my possible.

MRS. MEGAN. I could get an unfurnished room if [*she slides her eyes round at* WELLWYN] I 'ad the money to furnish it.

BERTLEY. But suppose I can induce your husband to forgive you, and take you back?

MRS. MEGAN. [*Shaking her head.*] 'E'd 'it me.

BERTLEY. I said to forgive.

MRS. MEGAN. That wouldn't make no difference. [*With a flash at* BERTLEY.] An' I ain't forgiven him!

BERTLEY. That is sinful.

MRS. MEGAN. *I'm* a Catholic.

BERTLEY. My good child, what difference does that make?

FERRAND. Monsieur, if I might interpret for her.

[BERTLEY *silences him with a gesture.*

MRS. MEGAN. [*Sliding her eyes towards* WELLWYN.] If I 'ad the money to buy some fresh stock.

BERTLEY. Yes; yes; never mind the money. What I want to find in you both, is repentance.

MRS. MEGAN. [*With a flash up at him.*] I can't get me livin' off of repentin'.

BERTLEY. Now, now! Never say what you know to be wrong.

FERRAND. Monsieur, her soul is very simple.

BERTLEY. [*Severely*.] I do not know, sir, that we shall get any great assistance from your views. In fact, one thing is clear to me, she must discontinue your acquaintanceship at once.

FERRAND. Certainly, Monsieur. We have no serious intentions.

BERTLEY. All the more shame to you, then!

FERRAND. Monsieur, I see perfectly your point of view. It is very natural. [*He bows and is silent.*

MRS. MEGAN. I don't want '*im* hurt 'cos o' me. Megan'll get his mates to belt him—bein' foreign like he is.

BERTLEY. Yes, never mind that. It's *you* I'm thinking of.

MRS. MEGAN. I'd sooner they'd hit *me*.

WELLWYN. [*Suddenly*.] Well said, my child!

MRS. MEGAN. 'Twasn't his fault.

FERRAND. [*Without irony—to* WELLWYN.] I cannot accept that Monsieur. The blame—it is all mine.

ANN. [*Entering suddenly from the house*.] Daddy, they're having an awful——!

[*The voices of* PROFESSOR CALWAY *and* SIR THOMAS HOXTON *are distinctly heard.*

CALWAY. The question is a much wider one, Sir Thomas.

HOXTON. As wide as you like, you'll never——

[WELLWYN *pushes* ANN *back into the house and closes the door behind her. The voices are still faintly heard arguing on the threshold.*

BERTLEY. Let me go in here a minute, Wellwyn. I must finish speaking to her. [*He motions* MRS. MEGAN *towards the model's room.*] We can't leave the matter thus.

FERRAND. [*Suavely.*] Do you desire my company, Monsieur?

> [BERTLEY, *with a prohibitive gesture of his hand, shepherds the reluctant* MRS. MEGAN *into the model's room.*

WELLWYN. [*Sorrowfully.*] You shouldn't have done this, Ferrand. It wasn't the square thing.

FERRAND. [*With dignity.*] Monsieur, I feel that I am in the wrong. It was stronger than me.

> [*As he speaks,* SIR THOMAS HOXTON *and* PROFESSOR CALWAY *enter from the house. In the dim light, and the full cry of argument, they do not notice the figures at the fire.* SIR THOMAS HOXTON *leads towards the street door.*

HOXTON. No, sir, I repeat, if the country once commits itself to your views of reform, it's as good as doomed.

CALWAY. I seem to have heard that before, Sir Thomas. And let me say at once that your hitty-missy cart-load of bricks *régime*——

HOXTON. Is a deuced sight better, sir, than your grand-motherly methods. What the old fellow wants is a shock! With all this socialistic molly-coddling, you're losing sight of the individual.

CALWAY. [*Swiftly.*] You, sir, with your "devil take the hindmost," have never even seen him.

> [SIR THOMAS HOXTON, *throwing back a gesture of disgust, steps out into the night, and falls heavily.*

Professor Calway, *hastening to his rescue,*
falls more heavily still.

[Timson, *momentarily roused from slumber on the*
doorstep, sits up.

Hoxton. [*Struggling to his knees.*] Damnation!

Calway. [*Sitting.*] How simultaneous!

[Wellwyn *and* Ferrand *approach hastily.*

Ferrand. [*Pointing to* Timson.] Monsieur, it was
true, it seems.   They had lost sight of the individual.

[*A Policeman has appeared under the street lamp.*
He picks up Hoxton's *hat.*

Constable. Anything wrong, sir?

Hoxton. [*Recovering his feet.*] Wrong?   Great Scott!
Constable!   Why do you let things lie about in the
street like this?   Look here, Wellwyn!

[*They all scrutinize* Timson.

Wellwyn. It's only the old fellow whose reform
you were discussing.

Hoxton. How did he come here?

Constable. Drunk, sir. [*Ascertaining* Timson *to be*
in the street.] Just off the premises, by good luck.
Come along, father.

Timson. [*Assisted to his feet—drowsily.*] Cert'nly, by
no means; take my arm.

[*They move from the doorway.* Hoxton *and*
Calway *re-enter, and go towards the fire.*

Ann. [*Entering from the house.*] What's happened?

Calway. Might we have a brush?

Hoxton. [*Testily.*] Let it dry!

[*He moves to the fire and stands before it.* PRO-
FESSOR CALWAY *following stands a little behind
him.* ANN *returning begins to brush the* PRO-
FESSOR'S *sleeve.*

WELLWYN. [*Turning from the door, where he has stood
looking after the receding* TIMSON.] Poor old Timson!

FERRAND. [*Softly.*] Must be philosopher, Monsieur!
They will but run him in a little.

[*From the model's room* MRS. MEGAN *has come
out, shepherded by* CANON BERTLEY.

BERTLEY. Let's see, your Christian name is——.

MRS. MEGAN. Guinevere.

BERTLEY. Oh! Ah! Ah! Ann, take Gui—— take
our little friend into the study a minute: I am going to
put her into service. We shall make a new woman of
her, yet.

ANN. [*Handing* CANON BERTLEY *the brush, and turning to* MRS. MEGAN.] Come on!

[*She leads into the house, and* MRS. MEGAN *follows
stolidly.*

BERTLEY. [*Brushing* CALWAY'S *back.*] Have you
fallen?

CALWAY. Yes.

BERTLEY. Dear me! How was that?

HOXTON. That old ruffian drunk on the doorstep.
Hope they'll give him a sharp dose!   These rag-tags!

[*He looks round, and his angry eyes light by chance
on* FERRAND.

FERRAND. [*With his eyes on* HOXTON—*softly.*] Mon-

sieur, something tells me it is time I took the road
again.

WELLWYN. [*Fumbling out a sovereign.*] Take this,
then!

FERRAND. [*Refusing the coin.*] Non, Monsieur. To
abuse 'ospitality is not in my character.

BERTLEY. We must not despair of anyone.

HOXTON. Who talked of despairing? Treat him, as
I say, and you'll see!

CALWAY. The interest of the State——

HOXTON. The interest of the individual citizen
sir——

BERTLEY. Come! A little of both, a little of both!

> [*They resume their brushing.*

FERRAND. You are now debarrassed of us three,
Monsieur. I leave you instead—these sirs. [*He points.*]
Au revoir, Monsieur! [*Motioning towards the fire.*]
'Appy New Year!

> [*He slips quietly out.* WELLWYN, *turning, con-
> templates the three reformers. They are all now
> brushing away, scratching each other's backs,
> and gravely hissing. As he approaches them,
> they speak with a certain unanimity.*

HOXTON. My theory——!

CALWAY. My theory——!

BERTLEY. My theory——!

> [*They stop surprised.* WELLWYN *makes a gesture
> of discomfort, as they speak again with still more
> unanimity.*

HOXTON. My——!
CALWAY. My——!
BERTLEY. My——!

> [*They stop in greater surprise.*
> *The stage is blotted dark.*

Curtain.

ACT III

It is the first of April—a white spring day of gleams and driving showers. The street door of WELLWYN'S *studio stands wide open, and, past it, in the street, the wind is whirling bits of straw and paper bags. Through the door can be seen the butt end of a stationary furniture van with its flap let down. To this van three humble-men in shirt sleeves and aprons, are carrying out the contents of the studio. The hissing samovar, the tea-pot, the sugar, and the nearly empty decanter of rum stand on the low round table in the fast-being-gutted room.* WELLWYN *in his ulster and soft hat, is squatting on the little stool in front of the blazing fire, staring into it, and smoking a hand-made cigarette. He has a moulting air. Behind him the humble-men pass, embracing busts and other articles of vertu.*

CHIEF H'MAN. [*Stopping, and standing in the attitude of expectation.*] We've about pinched this little lot, sir. Shall we take the—reservoir?

[*He indicates the samovar.*

WELLWYN. Ah! [*Abstractedly feeling in his pockets, and finding coins.*] Thanks—thanks—heavy work, I'm afraid.

59

H'MAN. [*Receiving the coins—a little surprised and a good deal pleased.*] Thank'ee, sir. Much obliged, I'm sure. We'll 'ave to come back for this. [*He gives the dais a vigorous push with his foot.*] Not a fixture, as I understand. Perhaps you'd like us to leave these 'ere for a bit.   [*He indicates the tea things.*

WELLWYN. Ah! do.

> [*The humble-men go out. There is the sound of horses being started, and the butt end of the van disappears.* WELLWYN *stays on his stool, smoking and brooding over the fire. The open doorway is darkened by a figure.* CANON BERT-LEY *is standing there.*

BERTLEY. Wellwyn! [WELLWYN *turns and rises.*] It's ages since I saw you. No idea you were moving. This is very dreadful.

WELLWYN. Yes, Ann found this—too exposed. That tall house in Flight Street—we're going there. Seventh floor.

BERTLEY. Lift?

> [WELLWYN *shakes his head.*

BERTLEY. Dear me! No lift? Fine view, no doubt. [WELLWYN *nods.*] You'll be greatly missed.

WELLWYN. So Ann thinks. Vicar, what's become of that little flower-seller I was painting at Christmas? You took her into service.

BERTLEY. Not we—exactly! Some dear friends of ours. Painful subject!

WELLWYN. Oh!

BERTLEY. Yes. She got the footman into trouble.

WELLWYN. Did she, now?

BERTLEY. Disappointing. I consulted with Calway, and he advised me to try a certain institution. We got her safely in—excellent place; but, d'you know, she broke out three weeks ago. And since—I've heard— [*he holds his hands up*] hopeless, I'm afraid—quite!

WELLWYN. I *thought* I saw her last night. You can't tell me her address, I suppose?

BERTLEY. [*Shaking his head.*] The husband too has quite passed out of my ken. He betted on horses, you remember. I'm sometimes tempted to believe there's nothing for some of these poor folk but to pray for death.

> [ANN *has entered from the house. Her hair hangs from under a knitted cap. She wears a white wool jersey, and a loose silk scarf.*

BERTLEY. Ah! Ann. I was telling your father of that poor little Mrs. Megan.

ANN. Is she dead?

BERTLEY. Worse I fear. By the way—what became of her accomplice?

ANN. We haven't seen him since. [*She looks searchingly at* WELLWYN.] At least—have *you*—Daddy?

WELLWYN. [*Rather hurt.*] No, my dear; I have not.

BERTLEY. And the—old gentleman who drank the rum?

ANN. He got fourteen days. It was the fifth time.

BERTLEY. Dear me!

ANN. When he came out he got more drunk than ever. Rather a score for Professor Calway, wasn't it?

BERTLEY. I remember. He and Sir Thomas took a kindly interest in the old fellow.

ANN. Yes, they fell over him. The Professor got him into an Institution.

BERTLEY. Indeed!

ANN. He was perfectly sober all the time he was there.

WELLWYN. My dear, they only allow them milk.

ANN. Well, anyway, he was reformed.

WELLWYN. Ye—yes!

ANN. [*Terribly.*] Daddy! You've been seeing him!

WELLWYN. [*With dignity.*] My dear, I have not.

ANN. How do you know, then?

WELLWYN. Came across Sir Thomas on the Embankment yesterday; told me old Timson had been had up again for sitting down in front of a brewer's dray.

ANN. Why?

WELLWYN. Well, you see, as soon as he came out of the what d'you call 'em, he got drunk for a week, and it left him in low spirits.

BERTLEY. Do you mean he deliberately sat down, with the intention—of—er?

WELLWYN. Said he was tired of life, but they didn't believe him.

ANN. Rather a score for Sir Thomas! I suppose he'd told the Professor? What did *he* say?

WELLWYN. Well, the Professor said [*with a quick glance at* BERTLEY] he felt there was nothing for some of these poor devils but a lethal chamber.

BERTLEY. [*Shocked.*] Did he really!

> [*He has not yet caught* WELLWYN'S *glance.*

WELLWYN. And Sir Thomas agreed. Historic occasion. And you, Vicar—H'm!

> [BERTLEY *winces.*

ANN. [*To herself.*] Well, there isn't.

BERTLEY. And yet! Some good in the old fellow, no doubt, if one could put one's finger on it. [*Preparing to go.*] You'll let us know, then, when you're settled. What was the address? [WELLWYN *takes out and hands him a card.*] Ah! yes. Good-bye, Ann. Good-bye, Wellwyn. [*The wind blows his hat along the street.*] What a wind!

> [*He goes, pursuing.*

ANN. [*Who has eyed the card askance.*] Daddy, have you told those other two where we're going?

WELLWYN. Which other two, my dear?

ANN. The Professor and Sir Thomas.

WELLWYN. Well, Ann, naturally I——

ANN. [*Jumping on to the dais with disgust.*] Oh, dear! When I'm trying to get you away from all this atmosphere. I don't so much mind the Vicar knowing, because he's got a weak heart——

> [*She jumps off again.*

WELLWYN. [*To himself.*] Seventh floor! I felt there was something.

ANN. [*Preparing to go.*] I'm going round now. But you must stay here till the van comes back. And don't forget you tipped the men after the first load.

WELLWYN. Oh! yes, yes. [*Uneasily.*] Good sorts they look, those fellows!

ANN. [*Scrutinising him.*] What have you done?

WELLWYN. Nothing, my dear, really——!

ANN. What?

WELLWYN. I—I rather think I may have tipped them twice.

ANN. [*Drily.*] Daddy! If it *is* the first of April, it's not necessary to make a fool of *oneself*. That's the last time you ever do these ridiculous things. [WELL-WYN *eyes her askance.*] I'm going to see that you spend your money on yourself. You needn't look at me like that! I *mean* to. As soon as I've got you away from here, and all—these——

WELLWYN. Don't rub it in, Ann!

ANN. [*Giving him a sudden hug—then going to the door—with a sort of triumph.*] Deeds, not words, Daddy!

> [*She goes out, and the wind catching her scarf blows it out beneath her firm young chin. WELL-WYN returning to the fire, stands brooding, and gazing at his extinct cigarette.*

WELLWYN. [*To himself.*] Bad lot—low type! No method! No theory!

> [*In the open doorway appear FERRAND and MRS. MEGAN. They stand, unseen, looking at him. FERRAND is more ragged, if possible, than on Christmas Eve. His chin and cheeks are clothed in a reddish golden beard. MRS. MEGAN'S dress is not so woe-begone, but her face is white, her eyes dark-circled. They whisper. She slips back into the shadow of the doorway. WELL-*

WYN *turns at the sound, and stares at* FERRAND *in amazement.*

FERRAND. [*Advancing.*] Enchanted to see you, Monsieur. [*He looks round the empty room.*] You are leaving?

WELLWYN. [*Nodding—then taking the young man's hand.*] How goes it?

FERRAND. [*Displaying himself, simply.*] As you see, Monsieur. I have done of my best. It still flies from me.

WELLWYN. [*Sadly—as if against his will.*] Ferrand, it will always fly.

[*The young foreigner shivers suddenly from head to foot; then controls himself with a great effort.*

FERRAND. Don't say that, Monsieur! It is too much the echo of my heart.

WELLWYN. Forgive me! I didn't mean to pain you.

FERRAND. [*Drawing nearer the fire.*] That old cabby, Monsieur, you remember—they tell me, he nearly succeeded to gain happiness the other day.

[WELLWYN *nods.*

FERRAND. And those Sirs, so interested in him, with their theories? He has worn them out? [WELLWYN *nods.*] That goes without saying. And now they wish for him the lethal chamber.

WELLWYN. [*Startled.*] How did you know that?

[*There is silence.*

FERRAND. [*Staring into the fire.*] Monsieur, while I was on the road this time I fell ill of a fever. It seemed to me in my illness that I saw the truth—how I was wasting in this world—I would never be good for any

one—nor any one for me—all would go by, and I never
of it—fame, and fortune, and peace, even the necessities of life, ever mocking me.

> [*He draws closer to the fire, spreading his fingers
> to the flame.   And while he is speaking, through
> the doorway* MRS. MEGAN *creeps in to listen.*

FERRAND. [*Speaking on into the fire.*] And I saw,
Monsieur, so plain, that I should be vagabond all my
days, and my days short, I dying in the end the death
of a dog.   I saw it all in my fever—clear as that flame
—there was nothing for us others, but the herb of death.
[WELLWYN *takes his arm and presses it.*] And so, Monsieur, I *wished* to die.   I told no one of my fever.   I
lay out on the ground—it was verree cold.   But they
would not let me die on the roads of their parishes—
they took me to an Institution, Monsieur, I looked in
their eyes while I lay there, and I saw more clear than
the blue heaven that they thought it best that I should
die, although they would not let me.   Then Monsieur,
naturally my spirit rose, and I said: "So much the
worse for you.   I will live a little more."   One is made
like that!   Life is sweet, Monsieur.

WELLWYN. Yes, Ferrand; Life is sweet.

FERRAND. That little girl you had here, Monsieur—
[WELLWYN *nods.*] in her too there is something of wild-
savage.   She must have joy of life.   I have seen her
since I came back.   She has embraced the life of joy.
It is not quite the same thing. [*He lowers his voice.*] She
is lost, Monsieur, as a stone that sinks in water.   I can
see, if she cannot. [*As* WELLWYN *makes a movement of*

distress.] Oh! I am not to blame for that, Monsieur.
It had well begun before I knew her.

WELLWYN. Yes, yes—I was afraid of it, at the time.

[MRS. MEGAN *turns silently, and slips away.*

FERRAND. I do my best for her, Monsieur, but look
at me! Besides, I am not good for her—it is not good
for simple souls to be with those who see things clear.
For the great part of mankind, to see anything—is
fatal.

WELLWYN. Even for you, it seems.

FERRAND. No, Monsieur. To be so near to death
has done me good; I shall not lack courage any more
till the wind blows on my grave. Since I saw you,
Monsieur, I have been in three Institutions. They are
palaces. One may eat upon the floor—though it is
true—for Kings—they eat too much of skilly there.
One little thing they lack—those palaces. It is under-
standing of the 'uman heart. In them tame birds
pluck wild birds naked.

WELLWYN. They mean well.

FERRAND. Ah! Monsieur, I am loafer, waster—
what you like—for all that [*bitterly*] poverty is my only
crime. If I were rich, should I not be simply veree
original, 'ighly respected, with soul above commerce,
travelling to see the world? And that young girl,
would she not be "that charming ladee," "veree *chic*,
you know!" And the old Tims—good old-fashioned
gentleman—drinking his liquor well. *Eh! bien*—what
are we now? Dark beasts, despised by all. That is
life, Monsieur.   [*He stares into the fire.*

WELLWYN. We're our own enemies, Ferrand. I can afford it—you can't. Quite true!

FERRAND. [*Earnestly.*] Monsieur, do you know this? You are the sole being that can do us good—we hopeless ones.

WELLWYN. [*Shaking his head.*] Not a bit of it; I'm hopeless too.

FERRAND. [*Eagerly.*] Monsieur, it is just that. You *understand*. When we are with you we feel something —here—[*he touches his heart.*] If I had one prayer to make, it would be, Good God, give me to understand! Those sirs, with their theories, they can clean our skins and chain our 'abits—that soothes for them the æsthetic sense; it gives them too their good little importance. But our spirits they cannot touch, for they nevare understand. Without that, Monsieur, all is dry as a parched skin of orange.

WELLWYN. Don't be so bitter. Think of all the work they do!

FERRAND. Monsieur, of their industry I say nothing. They do a good work while they attend with their theories to the sick and the tame old, and the good unfortunate deserving. Above all to the little children. But, Monsieur, when all is done, there are always us hopeless ones. What can they do with me, Monsieur, with that girl, or with that old man? Ah! Monsieur, we, too, 'ave our qualities, we others—it wants you courage to undertake a career like mine, or like that young girl's. We wild ones—we know a thousand times more of life than ever will those sirs. They waste their time trying to make rooks white. Be kind to us if you will, or let us alone like Mees Ann, but do not try to change our skins. Leave us to live, or leave us to die when we like in the free air. If you do not wish of us, you have but to shut your pockets and your doors —we shall die the faster.

WELLWYN. [*With agitation.*] But that, you know— we can't do—now can we?

FERRAND. If you cannot, how is it our fault? The harm we do to others—is it so much? If I am criminal, dangerous—shut me up! I would not pity myself— nevare. But we in whom something moves—like that flame, Monsieur, that *cannot* keep still—we others— we are not many—that must have motion in our lives, do not let them make us prisoners, with their theories, because we are not like them—it is life itself they would enclose! [*He draws up his tattered figure, then bending over the fire again.*] I ask your pardon; I am talking. If I could smoke, Monsieur!

[WELLWYN *hands him a tobacco pouch; and he rolls a cigarette with his yellow-stained fingers.*

FERRAND. The good God made me so that I would rather walk a whole month of nights, hungry, with the stars, than sit one single day making round business on an office stool! It is not to my advantage. I cannot help it that I am a vagabond. What would you have? It is stronger than me. [*He looks suddenly at* WELLWYN.] Monsieur, I say to you things I have never said.

WELLWYN. [*Quietly.*] Go on, go on. [*There is silence.*

FERRAND. [*Suddenly.*] Monsieur! Are you really English? The English are so civilised.

WELLWYN. And am I not?

FERRAND. You treat me like a brother.

[WELLWYN *has turned towards the street door at a sound of feet, and the clamour of voices.*

TIMSON. [*From the street.*] Take her in 'ere. I knows 'im.

[*Through the open doorway come a* POLICE CON-STABLE *and a* LOAFER, *bearing between them the limp white-faced form of* MRS. MEGAN, *hatless and with drowned hair, enveloped in the police-man's waterproof. Some curious persons bring up the rear, jostling in the doorway, among whom is* TIMSON *carrying in his hands the policeman's dripping waterproof leg pieces.*

FERRAND. [*Starting forward.*] Monsieur, it is that little girl!

WELLWYN. What's happened? Constable! What's happened!

[*The* CONSTABLE *and* LOAFER *have laid the body down on the dais; with* WELLWYN *and* FER-RAND *they stand bending over her.*

CONSTABLE. 'Tempted sooicide, sir; but she hadn't been in the water 'arf a minute when I got hold of her. [*He bends lower.*] Can't understand her collapsin' like this.

WELLWYN. [*Feeling her heart.*] I don't feel anything.

FERRAND. [*In a voice sharpened by emotion.*] Let me try, Monsieur.

CONSTABLE. [*Touching his arm.*] You keep off, my lad.

WELLWYN. No, constable—let him. He's her friend.

CONSTABLE. [*Releasing* FERRAND—*to the* LOAFER.] Here you! Cut off for a doctor—sharp now! [*He pushes back the curious persons.*] Now then, stand away there, please—we can't have you round the body. Keep back—Clear out, now!

> [*He slowly moves them back, and at last shepherds them through the door and shuts it on them,* TIMSON *being last.*

FERRAND. The rum!

> [WELLWYN *fetches the decanter. With the little there is left* FERRAND *chafes the girl's hands and forehead, and pours some between her lips. But there is no response from the inert body.*

FERRAND. Her soul is still away, Monsieur!

> [WELLWYN, *seizing the decanter, pours into it tea and boiling water.*

CONSTABLE. It's never drownin', sir—her head was hardly under; I was on to her like knife.

FERRAND. [*Rubbing her feet.*] She has not yet her philosophy, Monsieur; at the beginning they often try. If she is dead! [*In a voice of awed rapture.*] What fortune!

CONSTABLE. [*With puzzled sadness.*] True enough, sir—that! We'd just begun to know 'er. If she 'as been taken—her best friends couldn't wish 'er better.

WELLWYN. [*Applying the decanter to her lips.*] Poor little thing! I'll try this hot tea.

FERRAND. [*Whispering.*] *La mort—le grand ami!*

WELLWYN. Look! Look at her! She's coming round!

> [*A faint tremor passes over* MRS. MEGAN'S *body.*
> *He again applies the hot drink to her mouth.*
> *She stirs and gulps.*

CONSTABLE. [*With intense relief.*] That's brave! Good lass! She'll pick up now, sir.

> [*Then, seeing that* TIMSON *and the curious persons*
> *have again opened the door, he drives them out,*
> *and stands with his back against it.* MRS.
> MEGAN *comes to herself.*

WELLWYN. [*Sitting on the dais and supporting her—*
as if to a child.] There you are, my dear. There, there—better now! That's right. Drink a little more of this tea.

> [MRS. MEGAN *drinks from the decanter.*

FERRAND. [*Rising.*] Bring her to the fire, Monsieur.

> [*They take her to the fire and seat her on the little*
> *stool. From the moment of her restored anima-*
> *tion* FERRAND *has resumed his air of cynical*
> *detachment, and now stands apart with arms*
> *folded, watching.*

WELLWYN. Feeling better, my child?

MRS. MEGAN. Yes.

WELLWYN. That's good. That's good. Now, how was it? Um?

MRS. MEGAN. I dunno. [*She shivers.*] I was standin' here just now when you was talkin', and when I heard 'im, it cam' over me to do it—like.

WELLWYN. Ah, yes *I* know.

MRS. MEGAN. I didn't seem no good to meself nor any one. But when I got in the water, I didn't want to any more. It was cold in there.

WELLWYN. Have you been having such a bad time of it?

MRS. MEGAN. Yes. And listenin' to him upset me. [*She signs with her head at* FERRAND.] I feel better now I've been in the water.   [*She smiles and shivers.*

WELLWYN. There, there! Shivery? Like to walk up and down a little?

          [*They begin walking together up and down.*

WELLWYN. Beastly when your head goes under?

MRS. MEGAN. Yes. It frightened me. I thought I wouldn't come up again.

WELLWYN. I know—sort of world without end, wasn't it? What did you think of, um?

MRS. MEGAN. I wished I 'adn't jumped—an' I thought of my baby—that died—and—[*in a rather surprised voice*] and I thought of d-dancin'.

          [*Her mouth quivers, her face puckers, she gives a choke and a little sob.*

WELLWYN. [*Stopping and stroking her.*] There, there —there!

          [*For a moment her face is buried in his sleeve, then she recovers herself.*

MRS. MEGAN. Then 'e got hold o' me, an' pulled me out.

WELLWYN. Ah! what a comfort—um?

MRS. MEGAN. Yes. The water got into me mouth.

[*They walk again.*] I wouldn't have gone to do it but for *him.* [*She looks towards* FERRAND.] His talk made me feel all funny, as if people wanted me to.

WELLWYN. My dear child! Don't think such things! As if anyone would——!

MRS. MEGAN. [*Stolidly.*] I thought they did. They used to look at me so sometimes, where I was before I ran away—I couldn't stop there, you know.

WELLWYN. Too cooped-up?

MRS. MEGAN. Yes. No life at all, it wasn't—not after sellin' flowers, I'd rather be doin' what I am.

WELLWYN. Ah! Well—it's all over, now! How d'you feel—eh? Better?

MRS. MEGAN. Yes. I feels all right now.

[*She sits up again on the little stool before the fire.*
WELLWYN. No shivers, and no aches; quite comfy?

MRS. MEGAN. Yes.

WELLWYN. That's a blessing. All well, now, Constable—-thank you!

CONSTABLE. [*Who has remained discreetly apart at the door—cordially.*] First rate, sir! That's capital! [*He approaches and scrutinises* MRS. MEGAN.] Right as rain, eh, my girl?

MRS. MEGAN. [*Shrinking a little.*] Yes.

CONSTABLE. That's fine. Then I think perhaps, for 'er sake, sir, the sooner we move on and get her a change o' clothin', the better.

WELLWYN. Oh! don't bother about that—I'll send round for my daughter—we'll manage for her here.

CONSTABLE. Very kind of you, I'm sure, sir. But [*with embarrassment*] she seems all right. She'll get every attention at the station.

WELLWYN. But I assure you, we don't mind at all; we'll take the greatest care of her.

CONSTABLE. [*Still more embarrassed.*] Well, sir, of course, I'm thinkin' of—— I'm afraid I can't depart from the usual course.

WELLWYN. [*Sharply.*] What! But—oh! No! No! That'll be all right, Constable! That'll be all right! I assure you.

CONSTABLE. [*With more decision.*] I'll have to charge her, sir.

WELLWYN. Good God! You don't mean to say the poor little thing has got to be——

CONSTABLE. [*Consulting with him.*] Well, sir, we can't get over the facts, can we? There it is! You know what sooicide amounts to—it's an awkward job.

WELLWYN. [*Calming himself with an effort.*] But look here, Constable, as a reasonable man—— This poor wretched little girl—*you* know what that life means better than anyone! Why! It's to her credit to try and jump out of it!

[*The* CONSTABLE *shakes his head.*

WELLWYN. You said yourself her best friends couldn't wish her better! [*Dropping his voice still more.*] Everybody feels it! The Vicar was here a few minutes ago saying the very same thing—the Vicar, Constable! [*The* CONSTABLE *shakes his head.*] Ah! now, look here, I know something of her. Nothing can be done with her. We all admit it. Don't you see? Well, then hang it—you needn't go and make fools of us all by——

FERRAND. Monsieur, it is the first of April.

CONSTABLE. [*With a sharp glance at him.*] Can't neglect me duty, sir; that's impossible.

WELLWYN. Look here! She—slipped. She's been telling me. Come, Constable, there's a good fellow. May be the making of her, this.

CONSTABLE. I quite appreciate your good 'eart, sir, an' you make it very 'ard for me—but, come now! I put it to you as a gentleman, would you go back on yer duty if you was me?

[WELLWYN *raises his hat, and plunges his fingers through and through his hair.*

WELLWYN. Well! God in heaven! Of all the d——d topsy-turvy——! Not a soul in the world wants her alive—and now she's to be prosecuted for trying to be where everyone wishes her.

CONSTABLE. Come, sir, come! Be a man!

[*Throughout all this* MRS. MEGAN *has sat stolidly before the fire, but as* FERRAND *suddenly steps forward she looks up at him.*

FERRAND. Do not grieve, Monsieur! This will give her courage. There is nothing that gives more courage than to see the irony of things. [*He touches* MRS. MEGAN's *shoulder.*] Go, my child; it will do you good.

[MRS. MEGAN *rises, and looks at him dazedly.*

CONSTABLE. [*Coming forward, and taking her by the hand.*] That's my good lass. Come along! We won't hurt you.

MRS. MEGAN. I don't want to go. They'll stare at me.

CONSTABLE. [*Comforting.*] Not they! I'll see to that.

WELLWYN. [*Very upset.*] Take her in a cab, Constable, if you must—for God's sake! [*He pulls out a shilling.*] Here!

CONSTABLE. [*Taking the shilling.*] I will, sir, certainly. Don't think I want to——

WELLWYN. No, no, I know. You're a good sort.

CONSTABLE. [*Comfortable.*] Don't you take on, sir. It's her first try; they won't be hard on 'er. Like as not only bind 'er over in her own recogs not to do it again. Come, my dear.

MRS. MEGAN. [*Trying to free herself from the policeman's cloak.*] I want to take this off. It looks so funny.

    [*As she speaks the door is opened by* ANN; *behind whom is dimly seen the form of old* TIMSON, *still heading the curious persons.*]

ANN. [*Looking from one to the other in amaze.*] What is it? What's happened? Daddy!

FERRAND. [*Out of the silence.*] It is nothing, Ma'-moiselle! She has failed to drown herself. They run her in a little.

WELLWYN. Lend her your jacket, my dear; she'll catch her death.

    [ANN, *feeling* MRS. MEGAN'S *arm, strips off her jacket, and helps her into it without a word.*]

CONSTABLE. [*Donning his cloak.*] Thank you, Miss— very good of you, I'm sure.

MRS. MEGAN. [*Mazed.*] It's warm!

> [*She gives them all a last half-smiling look, and passes with the* CONSTABLE *through the doorway.*]

FERRAND. That makes the third of us, Monsieur. We are not in luck. To wish us dead, it seems, is easier than to let us die.

> [*He looks at* ANN, *who is standing with her eyes fixed on her father.* WELLWYN *has taken from his pocket a visiting card.*]

WELLWYN. [*To* FERRAND.] Here quick; take this, run after her! When they've done with her tell her to come to us.

FERRAND. [*Taking the card, and reading the address.*] "No. 7, Haven House, Flight Street!" Rely on me, Monsieur—I will bring her myself to call on you. *Au revoir, mon bon Monsieur!*

> [*He bends over* WELLWYN'S *hand; then, with a bow to* ANN *goes out; his tattered figure can be seen through the window, passing in the wind.* WELLWYN *turns back to the fire. The figure of* TIMSON *advances into the doorway, no longer holding in either hand a waterproof leg-piece.*]

TIMSON. [*In a croaky voice.*] Sir!

WELLWYN. What—you, Timson?

TIMSON. On me larst legs, sir. 'Ere! You can see 'em for yerself! Shawn't trouble yer long.

WELLWYN. [*After a long and desperate stare.*] Not now—Timson—not now! Take this! [*He takes out another card, and hands it to* TIMSON.] Some other time.

TIMSON. [*Taking the card.*] Yer new address! You *are* a gen'leman.   [*He lurches slowly away.*

> [ANN *shuts the street door and sets her back against it. The rumble of the approaching van is heard outside. It ceases.*

ANN. [*In a fateful voice.*] Daddy! [*They stare at each other.*] Do you know what you've done? Given your card to those six rotters.

WELLWYN. [*With a blank stare.*] Six?

ANN. [*Staring round the naked room.*] What was the good of this?

WELLWYN. [*Following her eyes—very gravely.*] Ann! It is stronger than me.

> [*Without a word* ANN *opens the door, and walks straight out. With a heavy sigh,* WELLWYN *sinks down on the little stool before the fire. The three humble-men come in.*

CHIEF HUMBLE-MAN. [*In an attitude of expectation.*] This is the larst of it, sir.

WELLWYN. Oh! Ah! yes!

> [*He gives them money; then something seems to strike him, and he exhibits certain signs of vexation. Suddenly he recovers, looks from one to the other, and then at the tea things. A faint smile comes on his face.*

WELLWYN. You can finish the decanter.

> [*He goes out in haste.*

CHIEF HUMBLE-MAN. [*Clinking the coins.*] Third time of arskin'! April fool! Not 'arf! Good old pigeon!

SECOND HUMBLE-MAN. 'Uman being, *I* call 'im.

CHIEF HUMBLE-MAN. [*Taking the three glasses from the last packing-case, and pouring very equally into them.*] That's right.   Tell you wot, I'd never 'a touched this unless 'e'd told me to, I wouldn't—not with 'im.

SECOND HUMBLE-MAN. Ditto to that!   This is a bit of orl right! [*Raising his glass.*] Good luck!

THIRD HUMBLE-MAN. Same 'ere!

> [*Simultaneously they place their lips smartly against the liquor, and at once let fall their faces and their glasses.*

CHIEF HUMBLE-MAN. [*With great solemnity.*] Crikey! Bill!   *Tea!* . . .   'E's *got* us!

The stage is blotted dark.

Curtain.

THE MOB
A PLAY IN FOUR ACTS

PERSONS OF THE PLAY

STEPHEN MORE, *Member of Parliament*
KATHERINE, *his wife*
OLIVE, *their little daughter*
THE DEAN OF STOUR, *Katherine's uncle*
GENERAL SIR JOHN JULIAN, *her father*
CAPTAIN HUBERT JULIAN, *her brother*
HELEN, *his wife*
EDWARD MENDIP, *editor of "The Parthenon"*
ALAN STEEL, *More's secretary*
JAMES HOME, *architect*
CHARLES SHELDER, *solicitor* ⎱ *A deputation of More's*
MARK WACE, *bookseller* ⎰ *constituents*
WILLIAM BANNING, *manufacturer*
NURSE WREFORD
WREFORD (*her son*), *Hubert's orderly*
HIS SWEETHEART
THE FOOTMAN HENRY
A DOORKEEPER
SOME BLACK-COATED GENTLEMEN
A STUDENT
A GIRL

A MOB

ACT I.   *The dining-room of More's town house, evening.*
ACT II.   *The same, morning.*
ACT III.   SCENE I. *An alley at the back of a suburban theatre.*
   SCENE II. *Katherine's bedroom.*
ACT IV.   *The dining-room of More's house, late afternoon.*
AFTERMATH.   *The corner of a square, at dawn.*

Between ACTS I and II some days elapse.
Between ACTS II and III three months.
Between ACT III SCENE I and ACT III SCENE II no time.
Between ACTS III and IV a few hours.
Between ACTS IV and AFTERMATH an indefinite period.

CAST OF THE ORIGINAL PRODUCTION

AT THE

GAIETY THEATRE, MANCHESTER, MARCH 30, 1914

Stephen More	MILTON ROSMER
Katherine	IRENE ROOKE
Olive	PHYLLIS BOURKE
The Dean of Stour	LEONARD MUDIE
General Sir John Julian	HERBERT LOMAS
Captain Hubert Julian	WILLIAM HOME
Helen	HILDA BRUCE POTTER
Edward Mendip	D. LEWIN MANNERING
Alan Steel	ERIC BARBER
James Home	ARCHIBALD McCLEAN
Charles Shelder	PERCY FOSTER
Mark Wace	NAPIER BARRY
William Banning	CHARLES BIBBY
Nurse Wreford	MRS. A. B. TAPPING
Wreford	CECIL CALVERT
His Sweetheart	HILDA DAVIES
The Footman Henry	BASIL HOLMES
A Doorkeeper	ALFRED RUSSELL
A Student	ELLIS DEE
A Girl	MURIEL POPE

ACT I

*It is half-past nine of a July evening. In a dining-room
lighted by sconces, and apparelled in wall-paper,
carpet, and curtains of deep vivid blue, the large
French windows between two columns are open on to
a wide terrace, beyond which are seen trees in darkness, and distant shapes of lighted houses. On one
side is a bay window, over which curtains are partly
drawn. Opposite to this window is a door leading
into the hall. At an oval rosewood table, set with
silver, flowers, fruit, and wine, six people are seated
after dinner. Back to the bay window is* STEPHEN
MORE, *the host, a man of forty, with a fine-cut face,
a rather charming smile, and the eyes of an idealist;
to his right,* SIR JOHN JULIAN, *an old soldier, with
thin brown features, and grey moustaches; to* SIR
JOHN'S *right, his brother, the* DEAN OF STOUR, *a
tall, dark, ascetic-looking Churchman: to his right*
KATHERINE *is leaning forward, her elbows on the
table, and her chin on her hands, staring across at
her husband; to her right sits* EDWARD MENDIP, *a
pale man of forty-five, very bald, with a fine forehead, and on his clear-cut lips a smile that shows
his teeth; between him and* MORE *is* HELEN JULIAN,

1

a pretty dark-haired young woman, absorbed in thoughts of her own. The voices are tuned to the pitch of heated discussion, as the curtain rises.

THE DEAN. I disagree with you, Stephen; absolutely, entirely disagree.

MORE. I can't help it.

MENDIP. Remember a certain war, Stephen! Were your chivalrous notions any good, then? And, what was winked at in an obscure young Member is anathema for an Under Secretary of State. You can't afford——

MORE. To follow my conscience? That's new, Mendip.

MENDIP. Idealism can be out of place, my friend.

THE DEAN. The Government is dealing here with a wild lawless race, on whom I must say I think sentiment is rather wasted.

MORE. God made them, Dean.

MENDIP. I have my doubts.

THE DEAN. They have proved themselves faithless. We have the right to chastise.

MORE. If I hit a little man in the eye, and he hits me back, have I the right to *chastise* him?

SIR JOHN. We didn't begin this business.

MORE. What! With our missionaries and our trading?

THE DEAN. It is news indeed that the work of civilization may be justifiably met by murder. Have you forgotten Glaive and Morlinson?

SIR JOHN. Yes. And that poor fellow Groome and his wife?

MORE. They went into a wild country, against the feeling of the tribes, on their own business. What has the nation to do with the mishaps of gamblers?

SIR JOHN. We can't stand by and see our own flesh and blood ill-treated!

THE DEAN. Does our rule bring blessing—or does it not, Stephen?

MORE. Sometimes; but with all my soul I deny the fantastic superstition that our rule can benefit a people like this, a nation of one race, as different from our-selves as dark from light—in colour, religion, every mortal thing. We can only pervert their natural in-stincts.

THE DEAN. That to me is an unintelligible point of view.

MENDIP. Go into that philosophy of yours a little deeper, Stephen—it spells stagnation. There are no fixed stars on this earth. Nations *can't* let each other alone.

MORE. Big ones could let little ones alone.

MENDIP. If they could there'd be no big ones. My dear fellow, we know little nations are your hobby, but surely office should have toned you down.

SIR JOHN. I've served my country fifty years, and I say she is not in the wrong.

MORE. I hope to serve her fifty, Sir John, and I say she is.

MENDIP. There are moments when such things can't be said, More.

MORE. They'll be said by me to-night, Mendip.

MENDIP. In the House?

[MORE *nods.*

KATHERINE. Stephen!

MENDIP. Mrs. More, you mustn't let him. It's madness.

MORE. [*Rising*] You can tell people that to-morrow, Mendip. Give it a leader in *The Parthenon.*

MENDIP. Political lunacy! No man in your position has a right to fly out like this at the eleventh hour.

MORE. I've made no secret of my feelings all along. I'm against this war, and against the annexation we all know it will lead to.

MENDIP. My dear fellow! Don't be so Quixotic! We shall have war within the next twenty-four hours, and nothing you can do will stop it.

HELEN. Oh! No!

MENDIP. I'm afraid so, Mrs. Hubert.

SIR JOHN. Not a doubt of it, Helen.

MENDIP. [*To* MORE] And you mean to charge the windmill?

[MORE *nods.*

MENDIP. *C'est magnifique!*

MORE. I'm not out for advertisement.

MENDIP. You will get it!

MORE. Must speak the truth sometimes, even at that risk.

SIR JOHN. It is not the truth.

MENDIP. The greater the truth the greater the libel, and the greater the resentment of the person libelled.

THE DEAN. [*Trying to bring matters to a blander level*] My dear Stephen, even if you were right—which I deny—about the initial merits, there surely comes a point where the individual conscience must resign itself to the country's feeling. This has become a question of national honour.

SIR JOHN. Well said, James!

MORE. Nations are bad judges of their honour, Dean.

THE DEAN. I shall not follow you there.

MORE. No. It's an awkward word.

KATHERINE. [*Stopping* THE DEAN] Uncle James! Please!

[MORE *looks at her intently.*

SIR JOHN. So you're going to put yourself at the head of the cranks, ruin your career, and make me ashamed that you're my son-in-law?

MORE. Is a man only to hold beliefs when they're popular? *You've* stood up to be shot at often enough, Sir John.

SIR JOHN. Never by my country! Your speech will be in all the foreign press—trust 'em for seizing on anything against us. A show-up before other countries——!

MORE. You admit the show-up?

SIR JOHN. I do not, sir.

THE DEAN. The position has become impossible. The state of things out there must be put an end to once for all! Come, Katherine, back us up!

MORE. My country, right or wrong! Guilty—still my country!

MENDIP. That begs the question.

> KATHERINE *rises.* THE DEAN, *too, stands up.*

THE DEAN. [*In a low voice*] Quem Deus vult perdere——!

SIR JOHN. Unpatriotic!

MORE. I'll have no truck with tyranny.

KATHERINE. Father doesn't admit tyranny. Nor do any of us, Stephen.

> HUBERT JULIAN, *a tall soldier-like man, has come in.*

HELEN. Hubert!

> *She gets up and goes to him, and they talk together near the door.*

SIR JOHN. What in God's name is your idea? We've forborne long enough, in all conscience.

MORE. Sir John, we great Powers have got to change our ways in dealing with weaker nations. The very dogs can give us lessons—watch a big dog with a little one.

MENDIP. No, no, these things are not so simple as all that.

MORE. There's no reason in the world, Mendip, why the rules of chivalry should not apply to nations at least as well as to—dogs.

MENDIP. My dear friend, are you to become that hapless kind of outcast, a champion of lost causes?

MORE. This cause is not lost.

MENDIP. Right or wrong, as lost as ever was cause

in all this world. There was never a time when the word "patriotism" stirred mob sentiment as it does now. 'Ware "Mob," Stephen—'ware "Mob"!

MORE. Because general sentiment's against me, I—a public man—am to deny my faith? The point is not whether I'm right or wrong, Mendip, but whether I'm to sneak out of my conviction because it's unpopular.

THE DEAN. I'm afraid I must go. [*To* KATHERINE] Good-night, my dear! Ah! Hubert! [*He greets* HUBERT] Mr. Mendip, I go your way. Can I drop you?

MENDIP. Thank you. Good-night, Mrs. More. Stop him! It's perdition.

> *He and* THE DEAN *go out.* KATHERINE *puts her arm in* HELEN'S, *and takes her out of the room.* HUBERT *remains standing by the door.*

SIR JOHN. I knew your views were extreme in many ways, Stephen, but I never thought the husband of my daughter would be a Peace-at-any-price man!

MORE. I am not! But I prefer to fight some one my own size.

SIR JOHN. Well! I can only hope to God you'll come to your senses before you commit the folly of this speech. I must get back to the War Office. Good-night, Hubert.

HUBERT. Good-night, Father.

> SIR JOHN *goes out.* HUBERT *stands motionless, dejected.*

HUBERT. We've got our orders.

MORE. What? When d'you sail?

HUBERT. At once.

MORE. Poor Helen!

HUBERT. Not married a year; pretty bad luck! [MORE *touches his arm in sympathy*] Well! We've got to put feelings in our pockets. Look here, Stephen— don't make that speech! Think of Katherine—with the Dad at the War Office, and me going out, and Ralph and old George out there already! You can't trust your tongue when you're hot about a thing.

MORE. I must speak, Hubert.

HUBERT. No, no! Bottle yourself up for to-night. The next few hours 'll see it begin. [MORE *turns from him*] If you don't care whether you mess up your own career—don't tear Katherine in two!

MORE. You're not shirking *your* duty because of *your* wife.

HUBERT. Well! You're riding for a fall, and a god- less mucker it'll be. This'll be no picnic. We shall get some nasty knocks out there. Wait and see the feeling here when we've had a force or two cut up in those mountains. It's awful country. Those fellows have got modern arms, and are jolly good fighters. Do drop it, Stephen!

MORE. Must risk something, sometimes, Hubert— even in my profession!

> [*As he speaks,* KATHERINE *comes in.*

HUBERT. But it's hopeless, my dear chap—abso- lutely.

> MORE *turns to the window,* HUBERT *to his sister*
> *—then with a gesture towards* MORE, *as though*
> *to leave the matter to her, he goes out.*

KATHERINE. Stephen! Are you really going to speak? [*He nods*] I ask you not.

MORE. You know my feeling.

KATHERINE. But it's our own country. We can't stand apart from it. You won't stop anything—only make people hate you. I can't bear that.

MORE. I tell you, Kit, some one must raise a voice. Two or three reverses—certain to come—and the whole country will go wild. And one more little nation will cease to live.

KATHERINE. If you believe in your country, you must believe that the more land and power she has, the better for the world.

MORE. Is that your faith?

KATHERINE. Yes.

MORE. I respect it; I even understand it; but—I can't hold it.

KATHERINE. But, Stephen, your speech will be a rallying cry to all the cranks, and every one who has a spite against the country. They'll make you their figurehead. [MORE *smiles*] They *will*. Your chance of the Cabinet will go—you may even have to resign your seat.

MORE. Dogs will bark. These things soon blow over.

KATHERINE. No, no! If you once begin a thing, you always go on; and what earthly good?

MORE. History won't say: "And this they did without a single protest from their public men!"

KATHERINE. There are plenty who——

MORE. Poets?

KATHERINE. Do you remember that day on our honeymoon, going up Ben Lawers? You were lying on your face in the heather; you said it was like kissing a loved woman. There was a lark singing—you said that was the voice of one's worship. The hills were very blue; that's why we had blue here, because it was the best dress of our country. You *do* love her.

MORE. Love her!

KATHERINE. You'd have done this for me—then.

MORE. Would you have asked me—then, Kit?

KATHERINE. Yes. The country's *our* country! Oh! Stephen, think what it'll be like for me—with Hubert and the other boys out there. And poor Helen, and Father! I beg you not to make this speech.

MORE. Kit! This isn't fair. Do you want me to feel myself a cur?

KATHERINE. [*Breathless*] I—I—almost feel you'll be a cur to do it [*She looks at him, frightened by her own words. Then, as the footman* HENRY *has come in to clear the table—very low*] I ask you not!

　　　　　　　[*He does not answer, and she goes out.*

MORE [*To the servant*] Later, please, Henry, later!

　　　　The servant retires. MORE *still stands looking down at the dining-table; then putting his hand to his throat, as if to free it from the grip of his collar, he pours out a glass of water, and drinks it off. In the street, outside the bay window, two street musicians, a harp and a violin, have taken up their stand, and after some twangs and scrapes, break into music.* MORE *goes towards the sound, and draws aside one curtain. After a moment, he returns to the table, and takes up the notes of the speech. He is in an agony of indecision.*

MORE. A cur!

He seems about to tear his notes across. Then, changing his mind, turns them over and over, muttering. His voice gradually grows louder, till he is declaiming to the empty room the peroration of his speech.

MORE. . . . We have arrogated to our land the title Champion of Freedom, Foe of Oppression. Is that indeed a bygone glory? Is it not worth some sacrifice of our pettier dignity, to avoid laying another stone upon its grave; to avoid placing before the searchlight eyes of History the spectacle of yet one more piece of national cynicism? We are about to force our will and our dominion on a race that has always been free, that loves its country, and its independence, as much as ever we love ours. I cannot sit silent to-night and see this begin. As we are tender of our own land, so we should be of the lands of others. I love my country. It is because I love my country that I raise my voice. Warlike in spirit these people may be—but they have no chance against ourselves. And war on such, however agreeable to the blind moment, is odious to the future. The great heart of mankind ever beats in sense and sympathy with the weaker. It is against this great heart of mankind that we are going. In the name of Justice and Civilization we pursue this policy;

but by Justice we shall hereafter be judged, and by Civilization—condemned.

> *While he is speaking, a little figure has flown along the terrace outside, in the direction of the music, but has stopped at the sound of his voice, and stands in the open window, listening —a dark-haired, dark-eyed child, in a blue dressing-gown caught up in her hand. The street musicians, having reached the end of a tune, are silent.*

> *In the intensity of* MORE'S *feeling, a wine-glass, gripped too strongly, breaks and falls in pieces on to a finger-bowl. The child starts forward into the room.*

MORE. Olive!

OLIVE. Who were you speaking to, Daddy?

MORE. [*Staring at her*] The wind, sweetheart!

OLIVE. There isn't any!

MORE. What blew *you* down, then?

OLIVE. [*Mysteriously*] The music. Did the wind break the wine-glass, or did it come in two in your hand?

MORE. Now my sprite! Upstairs again, before Nurse catches you.   Fly! Fly!

OLIVE. Oh! no, Daddy! [*With confidential fervour*] It feels like things to-night!

MORE. You're right there!

OLIVE. [*Pulling him down to her, and whispering*] I *must* get back again in secret.   H'sh!

> *She suddenly runs and wraps herself into one of*

*the curtains of the bay window. A young man
enters, with a note in his hand.*

MORE. Hallo, Steel!

[*The street musicians have again begun to play.*

STEEL. From Sir John—by special messenger from
the War Office.

MORE. [*Reading the note*] "The ball is opened."

He stands brooding over the note, and STEEL *looks
at him anxiously. He is a dark, sallow, thin-
faced young man, with the eyes of one who can
attach himself to people, and suffer with them.*

STEEL. I'm glad it's begun, sir. It would have
been an awful pity to have made that speech.

MORE. You too, Steel!

STEEL. I mean, if it's actually started——

MORE. [*Tearing the note across*] Yes. Keep that to
yourself.

STEEL. Do you want me any more?

MORE *takes from his breast pocket some papers,
and pitches them down on the bureau.*

MORE. Answer these.

STEEL. [*Going to the bureau*] Fetherby was simply
sickening. [*He begins to write. Struggle has begun
again in* MORE] Not the faintest recognition that there
are two sides to it.

MORE *gives him a quick look, goes quietly to the
dining-table and picks up his sheaf of notes.
Hiding them with his sleeve, he goes back to
the window, where he again stands hesitating.*

STEEL. Chief gem: [*Imitating*] "We must show Impudence at last that Dignity is not asleep!"

MORE. [*Moving out on to the terrace*] Nice quiet night!

STELL. This to the Cottage Hospital—shall I say you will preside?

MORE. No.

> STEEL *writes; then looking up and seeing that* MORE *is no longer there, he goes to the window, looks to right and left, returns to the bureau, and is about to sit down again when a thought seems to strike him with consternation. He goes again to the window. Then snatching up his hat, he passes hurriedly out along the terrace. As he vanishes,* KATHERINE *comes in from the hall. After looking out on to the terrace she goes to the bay window; stands there listening; then comes restlessly back into the room.* OLIVE, *creeping quietly from behind the curtain, clasps her round the waist.*

KATHERINE. O my darling! How you startled me! What *are* you doing down here, you wicked little sinner!

OLIVE. I explained all that to Daddy. We needn't go into it again, need we?

KATHERINE. Where *is* Daddy?

OLIVE. Gone.

KATHERINE. When?

OLIVE. Oh! only just, and Mr. Steel went after him like a rabbit. [*The music stops*] They haven't been paid, you know.

KATHERINE. Now, go up at once. I can't think how you got down here.

OLIVE. I can. [*Wheedling*] If you pay them, Mummy, they're sure to play another.

KATHERINE. Well, give them that! One more only.

> *She gives* OLIVE *a coin, who runs with it to the bay window, opens the side casement, and calls to the musicians.*

OLIVE. Catch, please! And would you play just one more?

> *She returns from the window, and seeing her mother lost in thought, rubs herself against her.*

OLIVE. Have you got an ache?

KATHERINE. Right through me, darling!

OLIVE. Oh!

> [*The musicians strike up a dance.*

OLIVE. Oh! Mummy! I must just dance!

> *She kicks off her little blue shoes, and begins dancing. While she is capering* HUBERT *comes in from the hall. He stands watching his little niece for a minute, and* KATHERINE *looks at him.*

HUBERT. Stephen gone!

KATHERINE. Yes—stop, Olive!

OLIVE. Are you good at my sort of dancing, Uncle?

HUBERT. Yes, chick—awfully!

KATHERINE. Now, Olive!

> *The musicians have suddenly broken off in the middle of a bar. From the street comes the noise of distant shouting.*

OLIVE. Listen, Uncle! Isn't it a particular noise?

>HUBERT *and* KATHERINE *listen with all their might, and* OLIVE *stares at their faces.* HUBERT *goes to the window. The sound comes nearer. The shouted words are faintly heard:* "Pyper—war—our force crosses frontier—sharp fightin' —pyper."

KATHERINE. [*Breathless*] Yes! It is.

>*The street cry is heard again in two distant voices coming from different directions:* "War—pyper —sharp fightin' on the frontier—pyper."

KATHERINE. Shut out those ghouls!

>*As* HUBERT *closes the window,* NURSE WREFORD *comes in from the hall. She is an elderly woman endowed with a motherly grimness. She fixes* OLIVE *with her eye, then suddenly becomes conscious of the street cry.*

NURSE. Oh! don't say it's begun.

>[HUBERT *comes from the window.*

NURSE. Is the regiment to go, Mr. Hubert?

HUBERT. Yes, Nanny.

NURSE. Oh, dear! My boy!

KATHERINE. [*Signing to where* OLIVE *stands with wide eyes*] Nurse!

HUBERT. I'll look after him, Nurse.

NURSE. And him keepin' company. And you not married a year. Ah! Mr. Hubert, now do 'ee take care; you and him's both so rash.

HUBERT. Not I, Nurse!

>NURSE *looks long into his face, then lifts her finger, and beckons* OLIVE.

OLIVE. [*Perceiving new sensations before her, goes quietly*] Good-night, Uncle! Nanny, d'you know why I was obliged to come down? [*In a fervent whisper*] It's a secret! [*As she passes with* NURSE *out into the hall, her voice is heard saying,* "Do tell me all about the war."]

HUBERT. [*Smothering emotion under a blunt manner*] We sail on Friday, Kit. Be good to Helen, old girl.

KATHERINE. Oh! I wish——! Why—can't—women—fight?

HUBERT. Yes, it's bad for you, with Stephen taking it like this. But he'll come round now it's once begun.

> KATHERINE *shakes her head, then goes suddenly up to him, and throws her arms round his neck. It is as if all the feeling pent up in her were finding vent in this hug.*
>
> *The door from the hall is opened, and* SIR JOHN's *voice is heard outside:* "*All right, I'll find her.*"

KATHERINE. Father!

> [SIR JOHN *comes in.*

SIR JOHN. Stephen get my note? I sent it over the moment I got to the War Office.

KATHERINE. I expect so. [*Seeing the torn note on the table*] Yes.

SIR JOHN. They're shouting the news now. Thank God, I stopped that crazy speech of his in time.

KATHERINE. Have you stopped it?

SIR JOHN. What! He wouldn't be such a sublime donkey?

KATHERINE. I think that is just what he might be.
[*Going to the window*] We shall know soon.

> SIR JOHN, *after staring at her, goes up to* HUBERT.

SIR JOHN. Keep a good heart, my boy.   The country's first. [*They exchange a hand-squeeze.*]

> KATHERINE *backs away from the window.* STEEL
>   *has appeared there from the terrace, breathless
>   from running.*

STEEL. Mr. More back?

KATHERINE. No.   Has he spoken?

STEEL. Yes.

KATHERINE. Against?

STEEL. Yes.

SIR JOHN. What?   After!

> SIR JOHN *stands rigid, then turns and marches
>   straight out into the hall.   At a sign from
>   KATHERINE, HUBERT follows him.*

KATHERINE. Yes, Mr. Steel?

STEEL. [*Still breathless and agitated*] We were here
—he slipped away from me somehow.   He must have
gone straight down to the House.   I ran over, but
when I got in under the Gallery he was speaking already.   They expected something—I never heard it
so still there.   He gripped them from the first word—
deadly—every syllable.   It got some of those fellows.
But all the time, under the silence you could feel a—
sort of—of—current going round.   And then Sherratt
—I think it was—began it, and you saw the anger
rising in them; but he kept them down—his quietness!
The feeling!   I've never seen anything like it there.

Then there was a whisper all over the House that
fighting had begun.   And the whole thing broke out—
a regular riot—as if they could have killed him.   Some
one tried to drag him down by the coat-tails, but he
shook him off, and went on.   Then he stopped dead
and walked out, and the noise dropped like a stone.
The whole thing didn't last five minutes.   It *was* fine,
Mrs. More; like—like lava; he was the only cool person there.   I wouldn't have missed it for anything—
it was grand!

> MORE *has appeared on the terrace, behind* STEEL.

KATHERINE. Good-night, Mr. Steel.

STEEL. [*Startled*] Oh!—Good-night!

> *He goes out into the hall.* KATHERINE *picks up*
> OLIVE'S *shoes, and stands clasping them to her*
> *breast.* MORE *comes in.*

KATHERINE. You've cleared your conscience, then!
I didn't think you'd hurt me so.

> MORE *does not answer, still living in the scene he*
> *has gone through, and* KATHERINE *goes a little*
> *nearer to him.*

KATHERINE. I'm with the country, heart and soul,
Stephen.   I warn you.

> *While they stand in silence, facing each other, the*
> *footman,* HENRY, *enters from the hall.*

FOOTMAN. These notes, sir, from the House of Com-
mons.

KATHERINE. [*Taking them*] You can have the room
directly.

> [*The* FOOTMAN *goes out.*

More. Open them!

> Katherine *opens one after the other, and lets them fall on the table.*

More. Well?

Katherine. What you might expect. Three of your best friends. It's begun.

More. 'Ware Mob! [*He gives a laugh*] I must write to the Chief.

> Katherine *makes an impulsive movement towards him; then quietly goes to the bureau, sits down and takes up a pen.*

Katherine. Let me make the rough draft. [*She waits*] Yes?

More. [*Dictating*]

"July 15th.

"Dear Sir Charles,—After my speech to-night, embodying my most unalterable convictions [Katherine *turns and looks up at him, but he is staring straight before him, and with a little movement of despair she goes on writing*] I have no alternative but to place the resignation of my Under-Secretaryship in your hands. My view, my faith in this matter may be wrong—but I am surely right to keep the flag of my faith flying. I imagine I need not enlarge on the reasons——"

THE CURTAIN FALLS.

ACT II

*Before noon a few days later.   The open windows of the
dining-room let in the sunlight.   On the table a number of newspapers are littered.   HELEN is sitting
there, staring straight before her.   A newspaper boy
runs by outside calling out his wares.   At the sound
she gets up and goes out on to the terrace.   HUBERT
enters from the hall.   He goes at once to the terrace,
and draws HELEN into the room.*

HELEN. Is it true—what they're shouting?

HUBERT. Yes.   Worse than we thought.   They got
our men all crumpled up in the Pass—guns helpless.
Ghastly beginning.

HELEN. Oh, Hubert!

HUBERT. My dearest girl!

> HELEN *puts her face up to his.   He kisses her.
> Then she turns quickly into the bay window.
> The door from the hall has been opened, and
> the footman,* HENRY, *comes in, preceding*
> WREFORD *and his sweetheart.*

HENRY. Just wait here, will you, while I let Mrs.
More know.   [*Catching sight of* HUBERT] Beg pardon,
sir!

HUBERT. All right, Henry.   [*Off-hand*] Ah! Wreford!   [*The* FOOTMAN *withdraws*] So you've brought her

21

round. That's good! My sister'll look after her—
don't you worry! Got everything packed? Three
o'clock sharp.

WREFORD. [*A broad-faced soldier, dressed in khaki
with a certain look of dry humour, now dimmed—speaking
with a West Country burr*] That's right, zurr; all's
ready.

> HELEN *has come out of the window, and is quietly
> looking at* WREFORD *and the girl standing there
> so awkwardly.*

HELEN. [*Quietly*] Take care of him, Wreford.

HUBERT. We'll take care of each other, won't we,
Wreford?

HELEN. How long have you been engaged?

THE GIRL. [*A pretty, indeterminate young woman*]
Six months. [*She sobs suddenly.*

HELEN. Ah! He'll soon be safe back.

WREFORD. I'll owe 'em for this. [*In a low voice to
her*] Don't 'ee now! Don't 'ee!

HELEN. No! Don't cry, please!

> *She stands struggling with her own lips, then goes
> out on to the terrace,* HUBERT *following.* WRE-
> FORD *and his girl remain where they were,
> strange and awkward, she muffling her sobs.*

WREFORD. Don't 'ee go on like that, Nance; I'll
'ave to take you 'ome. That's silly, now we've a-come.
I might be dead and buried by the fuss you're makin'.
You've a-drove the lady away. See!

> *She regains control of herself as the door is opened
> and* KATHERINE *appears, accompanied by*

OLIVE, *who regards* WREFORD *with awe and curiosity, and by* NURSE, *whose eyes are red, but whose manner is composed.*

KATHERINE. My brother told me; so glad you've brought her.

WREFORD. Ye—as, M'. She feels me goin', a bit.

KATHERINE. Yes, yes! Still, it's for the country, isn't it?

THE GIRL. That's what Wreford keeps tellin' me. He've got to go—so it's no use upsettin' 'im. And of course I keep tellin' him I shall be all right.

NURSE. [*Whose eyes never leave her son's face*] And so you will.

THE GIRL. Wreford thought it 'd comfort him to know you were interested in me. 'E's so 'ot-headed I'm sure somethin' 'll come to 'im.

KATHERINE. We've all got some one going. Are you coming to the docks? We must send them off in good spirits, you know.

OLIVE. Perhaps he'll get a medal.

KATHERINE. Olive!

NURSE. You wouldn't like for him to be hanging back, one of them anti-patriot, stop-the-war ones.

KATHERINE. [*Quickly*] Let me see—I have your address. [*Holding out her hand to* WREFORD] We'll look after her.

OLIVE. [*In a loud whisper*] Shall I lend him my toffee?

KATHERINE. If you like, dear. [*To* WREFORD] Now

take care of my brother and yourself, and we'll take care of her.

WREFORD. Ye—as, M'.

> *He then looks rather wretchedly at his girl, as if the interview had not done so much for him as he had hoped. She drops a little curtsey.* WREFORD *salutes.*

OLIVE. [*Who has taken from the bureau a packet, places it in his hand*] It's very nourishing!

WREFORD. Thank you, miss.

> *Then, nudging each other, and entangled in their feelings and the conventions, they pass out, shepherded by* NURSE.

KATHERINE. Poor things!

OLIVE. What is an anti-patriot, stop-the-war one, Mummy?

KATHERINE. [*Taking up a newspaper*] Just a stupid name, dear—don't chatter!

OLIVE. But tell me just one weeny thing!

KATHERINE. Well?

OLIVE. Is Daddy one?

KATHERINE. Olive! How much do you know about this war?

OLIVE. They won't obey us properly. So we have to beat them, and take away their country. We *shall*, shan't we?

KATHERINE. Yes. But Daddy doesn't want us to; he doesn't think it fair, and he's been saying so. People are very angry with him.

OLIVE. Why isn't it fair? I suppose we're littler than them.

KATHERINE. No.

OLIVE. Oh! in history we always are. And we always win. That's why I like history. Which are *you* for, Mummy—us or them?

KATHERINE. Us.

OLIVE. Then I shall have to be. It's a pity we're not on the same side as Daddy. [KATHERINE *shudders*] Will they hurt him for not taking our side?

KATHERINE. I expect they will, Olive.

OLIVE. Then we shall have to be extra nice to him.

KATHERINE. If we can.

OLIVE. *I* can; I feel like it.

> HELEN *and* HUBERT *have returned along the terrace. Seeing* KATHERINE *and the child,* HELEN *passes on, but* HUBERT *comes in at the French window.*

OLIVE. [*Catching sight of him—softly*] Is Uncle Hubert going to the front to-day? [KATHERINE *nods*] But not grandfather?

KATHERINE. No, dear.

OLIVE. That's lucky for *them*, isn't it?

> HUBERT *comes in. The presence of the child gives him self-control.*

HUBERT. Well, old girl, it's good-bye. [*To* OLIVE] What shall I bring you back, chick?

OLIVE. Are there shops at the front? I thought it was dangerous.

HUBERT. Not a bit.

OLIVE. [*Disillusioned*] Oh!

KATHERINE. Now, darling, give Uncle a good hug.

> *Under cover of* OLIVE's *hug,* KATHERINE *repairs her courage.*

KATHERINE. The Dad and I'll be with you all in spirit.   Good-bye, old boy!

> *They do not dare to kiss, and* HUBERT *goes out very stiff and straight, in the doorway passing* STEEL, *of whom he takes no notice.* STEEL *hesitates, and would go away.*

KATHERINE. Come in, Mr. Steel.

STEEL. The deputation from Toulmin ought to be here, Mrs. More.   It's twelve.

OLIVE. [*Having made a little ball of newspaper—slyly*] Mr. Steel, catch!

> [*She throws, and* STEEL *catches it in silence.*

KATHERINE. Go upstairs, won't you, darling?

OLIVE. Mayn't I read in the window, Mummy? Then I shall see if any soldiers pass.

KATHERINE. No.   You can go out on the terrace a little, and then you must go up.

> [OLIVE *goes reluctantly out on to the terrace.*

STEEL. Awful news this morning of that Pass! And have you seen these? [*Reading from the newspaper*] "We will have no truck with the jargon of the degenerate who vilifies his country at such a moment.   The Member for Toulmin has earned for himself the contempt of all virile patriots." [*He takes up a second journal*] "There is a certain type of public man who, even at his own expense, cannot resist the itch to advertise himself. We would, at moments of national crisis, muzzle such persons, as we muzzle dogs that we suspect of incipient rabies. . . ." They're in full cry after him!

KATHERINE. I mind much more all the creatures who are always flinging mud at the country making him their hero suddenly! You know what's in his mind?

STEEL. Oh! We *must* get him to give up that idea of lecturing everywhere against the war, Mrs. More; we simply must.

KATHERINE. [*Listening*] The deputation's come. Go and fetch him, Mr. Steel. He'll be in his room, at the House.

> STEEL *goes out, and* KATHERINE *stands at bay.
> In a moment he opens the door again, to usher
> in the deputation; then retires. The four gentle-
> men have entered as if conscious of grave issues.
> The first and most picturesque is* JAMES HOME,
> *a thin, tall, grey-bearded man, with plentiful
> hair, contradictious eyebrows, and the half-shy,
> half-bold manners, alternately rude and over-
> polite, of one not accustomed to Society, yet
> secretly much taken with himself. He is dressed
> in rough tweeds, with a red silk tie slung through
> a ring, and is closely followed by* MARK WACE,
> *a waxy, round-faced man of middle-age, with
> sleek dark hair, traces of whisker, and a smooth
> way of continually rubbing his hands together,
> as if selling something to an esteemed customer.*

He is rather stout, wears dark clothes, with
a large gold chain. Following him comes
CHARLES SHELDER, a lawyer of fifty, with a
bald egg-shaped head, and gold pince-nez. He
has little side whiskers, a leathery, yellowish
skin, a rather kind but watchful and dubious
face, and when he speaks seems to have a plum
in his mouth, which arises from the pre-
ponderance of his shaven upper lip. Last of
the deputation comes WILLIAM BANNING, an
energetic-looking, square-shouldered, self-made
country-man, between fifty and sixty, with grey
moustaches, ruddy face, and lively brown eyes.

KATHERINE. How do you do, Mr. Home?

HOME. [*Bowing rather extravagantly over her hand, as
if to show his independence of women's influence*] Mrs.
More! We hardly expected—— This is an honour.

WACE. How do you do, Ma'am?

KATHERINE. And you, Mr. Wace?

WACE. Thank you, Ma'am, well indeed!

SHELDER. How d'you do, Mrs. More?

KATHERINE. Very well, thank you, Mr. Shelder.

BANNING. [*Speaking with a rather broad country
accent*] This is but a poor occasion, Ma'am.

KATHERINE. Yes, Mr. Banning. Do sit down, gentlemen.

*Seeing that they will not settle down while she is
standing, she sits at the table. They gradually
take their seats. Each member of the deputation in his own way is severely hanging back*

from any mention of the subject in hand; and
KATHERINE *as intent on drawing them to it.*

KATHERINE. My husband will be here in two minutes. He's only over at the House.

SHELDER. [*Who is of higher standing and education than the others*] Charming position—this, Mrs. More! So near the—er—Centre of—Gravity—um?

KATHERINE. I read the account of your second meeting at Toulmin.

BANNING. It's bad, Mrs. More—bad. There's no disguising it. That speech was moon-summer madness—Ah! it *was!* Take a lot of explaining away. Why did you let him, now? Why did you? Not your views, I'm sure!

He looks at her, but for answer she only compresses her lips.

BANNING. I tell you what hit me—what's hit the whole constituency—and that's his knowing we were over the frontier, fighting already, when he made it.

KATHERINE. What difference does it make if he did know?

HOME. Hitting below the belt—I should have thought—you'll pardon me!

BANNING. Till war's begun, Mrs. More, you're entitled to say what you like, no doubt—but after! That's going against your country. Ah! his speech was strong, you know—his speech was strong.

KATHERINE. He had made up his mind to speak. It was just an accident the news coming then.

[*A silence.*

Banning. Well, that's true, I suppose. What we really want is to make sure he won't break out again.

Home. Very high-minded, his views of course—but, some consideration for the common herd. You'll pardon me!

Shelder. We've come with the friendliest feelings, Mrs. More—but, you know, it won't do, this sort of thing!

Wace. We shall be able to smooth him down. Oh! surely.

Banning. We'd be best perhaps not to mention about his knowing that fighting had begun.

As he speaks, More enters through the French windows. They all rise.

More. Good-morning, gentlemen.

He comes down to the table, but does not offer to shake hands.

Banning. Well, Mr. More? You've made a woeful mistake, sir; I tell you to your face.

More. As everybody else does, Banning. Sit down again, please.

They gradually resume their seats, and More sits in Katherine's chair. She alone remains standing leaning against the corner of the bay window, watching their faces.

Banning. You've seen the morning's telegrams? I tell you, Mr. More—another reverse like that, and the flood will sweep you clean away. And I'll not blame it. It's only flesh and blood.

MORE. Allow for the flesh and blood in *me*, too, please.   When I spoke the other night it was not without a certain feeling here.   [*He touches his heart.*

BANNING. But your attitude's so sudden—you'd not been going that length when you were down with us in May.

MORE. Do me the justice to remember that even then I was against our policy.   It cost me three weeks' hard struggle to make up my mind to that speech. One comes slowly to these things, Banning.

SHELDER. Case of conscience?

MORE. Such things have happened, Shelder, even in politics.

SHELDER. You see, our ideals are naturally low— how different from yours!

[MORE *smiles.*
KATHERINE, *who has drawn near her husband, moves back again, as if relieved at this gleam of geniality.*   WACE *rubs his hands.*

BANNING. There's one thing you forget, sir.   We send you to Parliament, representing us; but you couldn't find six men in the whole constituency that would have bidden you to make that speech.

MORE. I'm sorry; but I can't help my convictions, Banning.

SHELDER. What was it the prophet was without in his own country?

BANNING. Ah! but we're not funning, Mr. More. I've never known feeling run so high.   The sentiment of both meetings was dead against you.   We've had showers of letters to headquarters. Some from very good men—very warm friends of yours.

SHELDER. Come now! It's not too late. Let's go back and tell them you won't do it again.

MORE. Muzzling order?

BANNING. [*Bluntly*] That's about it.

MORE. Give up my principles to save my Parliamentary skin. Then, indeed, they might call me a degenerate! [*He touches the newspapers on the table.*

KATHERINE *makes an abrupt and painful movement, then remains as still as before, leaning against the corner of the window-seat.*

BANNING. Well, well! I know. But we don't ask you to take your words back—we only want discretion in the future.

MORE. Conspiracy of silence! And have it said that a mob of newspapers have hounded me to it.

BANNING. They won't say that of *you*.

SHELDER. My dear More, aren't you rather dropping to our level? With your principles you ought not to care two straws what people say.

MORE. But I do. I can't betray the dignity and courage of public men. If popular opinion is to control the utterances of her politicians, then good-bye indeed to this country!

BANNING. Come now! I won't say that your views weren't sound enough before the fighting began. I've never liked our policy out there. But our blood's being spilled; and that makes all the difference. I don't suppose they'd want me exactly, but I'd be ready to go myself. We'd all of us be ready. And we can't have the man that represents us talking wild, until we've licked these fellows. That's it in a nutshell.

MORE. I understand your feeling, Banning. I tender you my resignation. I can't and won't hold on where I'm not wanted.

BANNING. No, no, no! Don't do that! [*His accent broader and broader*] You've 'ad your say, and there it is. Coom now! You've been our Member nine years, in rain and shine.

SHELDER. We want to keep you, More. Come! Give us your promise—that's a good man!

MORE. I don't make cheap promises. You ask too much.

        [*There is silence, and they all look at* MORE.

SHELDER. There are very excellent reasons for the Government's policy.

MORE. There are always excellent reasons for having your way with the weak.

SHELDER. My dear More, how can you get up any enthusiasm for those cattle-lifting ruffians?

MORE. Better lift cattle than lift freedom.

SHELDER. Well, all we'll ask is that you shouldn't go about the country, saying so.

MORE. But that is just what I must do.

        [*Again they all look at* MORE *in consternation.*

HOME. Not down our way, you'll pardon me.

WACE. Really—really, sir——

SHELDER. The time of crusades is past, More.

MORE. Is it?

BANNING. Ah! no, but we don't want to part with you, Mr. More. It's a bitter thing, this, after three elections. Look at the 'uman side of it! To speak ill of your country when there's been a disaster like this terrible business in the Pass. There's your own wife. I see her brother's regiment's to start this very afternoon. Come now—how must she feel?

> MORE *breaks away to the bay window. The* DEPUTATION *exchange glances.*

MORE. [*Turning*] To try to muzzle me like this—is going too far.

BANNING. We just want to put you out of temptation.

MORE. I've held my seat with you in all weathers for nine years. You've all been bricks to me. My heart's in my work, Banning; I'm not eager to undergo political eclipse at forty.

SHELDER. Just so—we don't want to see you in that quandary.

BANNING. It'd be no friendliness to give you a wrong impression of the state of feeling. Silence—till the bitterness is overpast; there's naught else for it, Mr. More, while you feel as you do. That tongue of yours! Come! You owe us something. You're a big man; it's the big view you ought to take.

MORE. I am trying to.

HOME. And what precisely is your view—you'll pardon my asking?

MORE. [*Turning on him*] Mr. Home—a great country such as ours—is trustee for the highest sentiments

of mankind.   Do these few outrages justify us in stealing the freedom of this little people?

BANNING. Steal their freedom!   That's rather running before the hounds.

MORE. Ah, Banning! now we come to it.   In your
hearts you're none of you for that—neither by force
nor fraud.   And yet you all know that we've gone in
there to stay, as we've gone into other lands—as all
we big Powers go into other lands, when they're little
and weak.   The Prime Minister's words the other
night were these: "If we are forced to spend this blood
and money now, we must never again be forced."
What does that mean but swallowing this country?

SHELDER. Well, and quite frankly, it'd be no bad
thing.

HOME. We don't want their wretched country—
we're forced.

MORE. We are *not* forced.

SHELDER. My dear More, what is civilization but
the logical, inevitable swallowing up of the lower by
the higher types of man?   And what else will it be
here?

MORE. We shall not agree there, Shelder; and we
might argue it all day.   But the point is, not whether
you or I are right—the point is: What is a man who
holds a faith with all his heart to do?   Please tell me.

[*There is a silence.*

BANNING. [*Simply*] I was just thinkin' of those poor
fellows in the Pass.

MORE. I can see them, as well as you, Banning.

But, imagine! Up in our own country—the Black Valley—twelve hundred foreign devils dead and dying —the crows busy over them—in our own country, our own valley—ours—ours—violated. Would you care about "the poor fellows" in *that* Pass?—Invading, stealing dogs! Kill them—kill them! You would, and I would, too!

> *The passion of those words touches and grips as no arguments could; and they are silent.*

MORE. Well! What's the difference out there? I'm not so inhuman as not to want to see this disaster in the Pass wiped out. But once that's done, in spite of my affection for you; my ambitions, and they're not few; [*Very low*] in spite of my own wife's feeling, I must be free to raise my voice against this war.

BANNING. [*Speaking slowly, consulting the others, as it were, with his eyes*] Mr. More, there's no man I respect more than yourself. I can't tell what they'll say down there when we go back; but I, for one, don't feel it in me to take a hand in pressing you farther against your faith.

SHELDER. We don't deny that—that you have a case of sorts.

WACE. No—surely.

SHELDER. A man should be free, I suppose, to hold his own opinions.

MORE. Thank you, Shelder.

BANNING. Well! well! We must take you as you are; but it's a rare pity; there'll be a lot of trouble——

> *His eyes light on* HOME, *who is leaning forward*

with hand raised to his ear, listening. Very faint, from far in the distance, there is heard a skirling sound. All become conscious of it, all listen.

HOME. [*Suddenly*] Bagpipes!

The figure of OLIVE *flies past the window, out on the terrace.* KATHERINE *turns, as if to follow her.*

SHELDER. Highlanders!   [*He rises.*

KATHERINE *goes quickly out on to the terrace. One by one they all follow to the window. One by one go out on to the terrace, till* MORE *is left alone. He turns to the bay window. The music is swelling, coming nearer.* MORE *leaves the window—his face distorted by the strife of his emotions. He paces the room, taking, in some sort, the rhythm of the march.*

Slowly the music dies away in the distance to a drum-tap and the tramp of a company. MORE *stops at the table, covering his eyes with his hands.*

The DEPUTATION *troop back across the terrace, and come in at the French windows. Their faces and manners have quite changed.* KATH-ERINE *follows them as far as the window.*

HOME. [*In a strange, almost threatening voice*] It won't do, Mr. More. Give us your word, to hold your peace!

SHELDER. Come! More.

WACE. Yes, indeed—indeed!

BANNING. We must have it.

MORE. [*Without lifting his head*] I—I——

> *The drum-tap of a regiment marching is heard.*

BANNING. Can you hear that go by, man—when your country's just been struck?

> *Now comes the scuffle and mutter of a following crowd.*

MORE. I give you——

> *Then, sharp and clear above all other sounds, the words:* "Give the beggars hell, boys!" "Wipe your feet on their dirty country!" "Don't leave 'em a gory acre!" *And a burst of hoarse cheering.*

MORE. [*Flinging up his head*] That's reality! By Heaven! No!

KATHERINE. Oh!

SHELDER. In that case, we'll go.

BANNING. You mean it? You lose us, then!

> [MORE *bows.*

HOME. Good riddance [*Venomously—his eyes darting between* MORE *and* KATHERINE]! Go and stump the country! Find out what they think of you! You'll pardon me!

> *One by one, without a word, only* BANNING *looking back, they pass out into the hall.* MORE *sits down at the table before the pile of newspapers.* KATHERINE, *in the window, never moves.* OLIVE *comes along the terrace to her mother.*

OLIVE. They *were* nice ones! Such a lot of dirty people following, and some quite clean, Mummy. [*Con-

*scious from her mother's face that something is very wrong,
she looks at her father, and then steals up to his side*]
Uncle Hubert's gone, Daddy; and Auntie Helen's crying.   And—look at Mummy!

> [MORE *raises his head and looks.*

OLIVE. Do be on our side!   Do!

> *She rubs her cheek against his.   Feeling that he
> does not rub his cheek against hers,* OLIVE
> *stands away, and looks from him to her mother in
> wonder.*

THE CURTAIN FALLS

ACT III

SCENE I

A cobble-stoned alley, without pavement, behind a sub-urban theatre. The tall, blind, dingy-yellowish wall of the building is plastered with the tattered remnants of old entertainment bills, and the words: "To Let," and with several torn, and one still virgin placard, containing this announcement: "Stop-the-War Meeting, October 1st. Addresses by STEPHEN MORE, Esq., and others." The alley is plentifully strewn with refuse and scraps of paper. Three stone steps, inset, lead to the stage door. It is a dark night, and a street lamp close to the wall throws all the light there is. A faint, confused murmur, as of distant hooting is heard. Suddenly a boy comes running, then two rough girls hurry past in the direction of the sound; and the alley is again deserted. The stage door opens, and a doorkeeper, poking his head out, looks up and down. He withdraws, but in a second reappears, preceding three black-coated gentlemen.

DOORKEEPER. It's all clear. You can get away down here, gentlemen. Keep to the left, then sharp to the right, round the corner.

41

THE THREE. [*Dusting themselves, and settling their ties*] Thanks, very much! Thanks!

FIRST BLACK-COATED GENTLEMAN. Where's More? Isn't he coming?

> *They are joined by a fourth black-coated* GENTLE-MAN.

FOURTH BLACK-COATED GENTLEMAN. Just behind. [*To the* DOORKEEPER] Thanks.

> *They hurry away. The* DOORKEEPER *retires. Another boy runs past. Then the door opens again* STEEL *and* MORE *come out.*
>
> MORE *stands hesitating on the steps; then turns as if to go back.*

STEEL. Come along, sir, come!

MORE. It sticks in my gizzard, Steel.

STEEL. [*Running his arm through* MORE'S, *and almost dragging him down the steps*] You owe it to the theatre people. [MORE *still hesitates*] We might be penned in there another hour; you told Mrs. More half-past ten; it'll only make her anxious. And she hasn't seen you for six weeks.

MORE. All right; don't dislocate my arm.

> *They move down the steps, and away to the left, as a boy comes running down the alley. Sighting* MORE, *he stops dead, spins round, and crying shrilly :* "'Ere 'e is! That's 'im! 'Ere 'e is!" *he bolts back in the direction whence he came.*

STEEL. Quick, sir, quick!

More. That is the end of the limit, as the foreign ambassador remarked.

Steel. [*Pulling him back towards the door*] Well! come inside again, anyway!

> *A number of men and boys, and a few young girls, are trooping quickly from the left. A motley crew, out for excitement; loafers, artisans, navvies; girls, rough or dubious. All in the mood of hunters, and having tasted blood. They gather round the steps displaying the momentary irresolution and curiosity that follows on a new development of any chase. More, on the bottom step, turns and eyes them.*

A Girl [*At the edge*] Which is 'im! The old 'un or the young?

> [More *turns, and mounts the remaining steps.*

Tall Youth. [*With lank black hair under a bowler hat*] You blasted traitor!

> More *faces round at the volley of jeering that follows; the chorus of booing swells, then gradually dies, as if they realized that they were spoiling their own sport.*

A Rough Girl. Don't frighten the poor feller!

> [*A girl beside her utters a shrill laugh.*

Steel. [*Tugging at* More's *arm*] Come along, sir.

More. [*Shaking his arm free—to the crowd*] Well, what do you want?

A Voice. Speech.

More. Indeed! That's new.

ROUGH VOICE. [*At the back of the crowd*] Look at his white liver. You can see it in his face.

A BIG NAVVY. [*In front*] Shut it! Give 'im a chanst!

TALL YOUTH. Silence for the blasted traitor?

> *A youth plays the concertina; there is laughter, then an abrupt silence.*

MORE. You shall have it in a nutshell!

A SHOPBOY. [*Flinging a walnut-shell which strikes* MORE *on the shoulder*] Here y'are!

MORE. Go home, and think! If foreigners invaded *us*, wouldn't you be fighting tooth and nail like those tribesmen, out there?

TALL YOUTH. Treacherous dogs! Why don't they come out in the open?

MORE. They fight the best way they can.

> *A burst of hooting is led by a soldier in khaki on the outskirts.*

MORE. My friend there in khaki led that hooting. I've never said a word against our soldiers. It's the Government I condemn for putting them to this, and the Press for hounding on the Government, and all of you for being led by the nose to do what none of you would do, left to yourselves.

> *The* TALL YOUTH *leads a somewhat unspontaneous burst of execration.*

MORE. I say not one of you would go for a weaker man.

VOICES IN THE CROWD.

ROUGH VOICE. Tork sense!

GIRL'S VOICE. He's gittin' at you!

TALL YOUTH'S VOICE. Shiny skunk!

A NAVVY. [*Suddenly shouldering forward*] Look 'ere, Mister! Don't you come gaffin' to those who've got mates out there, or it'll be the worse for you—you go 'ome!

COCKNEY VOICE. And git your wife to put cotton-wool in yer ears.

[*A spurt of laughter.*

A FRIENDLY VOICE. [*From the outskirts*] Shame! there! Bravo, More! Keep it up!

[*A scuffle drowns this cry.*

MORE. [*With vehemence*] Stop that! Stop that! You——!

TALL YOUTH. Traitor!

AN ARTISAN. Who black-legged?

MIDDLE-AGED MAN. Ought to be shot—backin' his country's enemies!

MORE. Those tribesmen are defending their homes.

TWO VOICES. Hear! hear!

[*They are hustled into silence.*

TALL YOUTH. Wind-bag!

MORE. [*With sudden passion*] Defending their homes! Not mobbing unarmed men!

[STEEL *again pulls at his arm.*

ROUGH. Shut it, or we'll do you in!

MORE. [*Recovering his coolness*] Ah! Do me in by all means! You'd deal such a blow at cowardly mobs as wouldn't be forgotten in your time.

STEEL. For God's sake, sir!

MORE. [*Shaking off his touch*] Well!

> *There is an ugly rush, checked by the fall of the foremost figures, thrown too suddenly against the bottom step. The crowd recoils.*
>
> *There is a momentary lull, and* MORE *stares steadily down at them.*

COCKNEY VOICE. Don't 'e speak well! What eloquence!

> *Two or three nutshells and a piece of orange-peel strike* MORE *across the face. He takes no notice.*

ROUGH VOICE. That's it! Give 'im some encouragement.

> *The jeering laughter is changed to anger by the contemptuous smile on* MORE'S *face.*

A TALL YOUTH. Traitor!

A VOICE. Don't stand there like a stuck pig.

A ROUGH. Let's 'ave 'im dahn off that!

> *Under cover of the applause that greets this, he strikes* MORE *across the legs with a belt.* STEEL *starts forward.* MORE, *flinging out his arm, turns him back, and resumes his tranquil staring at the crowd, in whom the sense of being foiled by this silence is fast turning to rage.*

THE CROWD. Speak up, or get down! Get off! Get away, there—or we'll make you! Go on!

> [MORE *remains immovable.*

A YOUTH. [*In a lull of disconcertion*] I'll make 'im speak! See!

> *He darts forward and spits, defiling* MORE'S
> *hand.* MORE *jerks it up as if it had been
> stung, then stands as still as ever. A spurt of
> laughter dies into a shiver of repugnance at the
> action. The shame is fanned again to fury by
> the sight of* MORE'S *scornful face.*

TALL YOUTH. [*Out of murmuring*] Shift! or you'll
get it!

A VOICE. Enough of your ugly mug!

A ROUGH. Give 'im one!

> *Two flung stones strike* MORE. *He staggers and
> nearly falls, then rights himself.*

A GIRL'S VOICE. Shame!

FRIENDLY VOICE. Bravo, More! Stick to it!

A ROUGH. Give 'im another!

A VOICE. No!

A GIRL'S VOICE. Let 'im alone! Come on, Billy,
this ain't no fun!

> *Still looking up at* MORE, *the whole crowd falls
> into an uneasy silence, broken only by the
> shuffling of feet. Then the* BIG NAVVY *in the
> front rank turns and elbows his way out to the
> edge of the crowd.*

THE NAVVY. Let 'im be!

> *With half-sullen and half-shamefaced acquies-
> cence the crowd breaks up and drifts back
> whence it came, till the alley is nearly empty.*

MORE. [*As if coming to, out of a trance—wiping his
hand and dusting his coat*] Well, Steel!

And followed by STEEL, *he descends the steps and moves away. Two policemen pass glancing up at the broken glass. One of them stops and makes a note.*

THE CURTAIN FALLS.

<h2 style="text-align:center">SCENE II</h2>

The window-end of KATHERINE'S *bedroom, panelled in cream-coloured wood. The light from four candles is falling on* KATHERINE, *who is sitting before the silver mirror of an old oak dressing-table, brushing her hair. A door, on the left, stands ajar. An oak chair against the wall close to a recessed window is all the other furniture. Through this window the blue night is seen, where a mist is rolled out flat amongst trees, so that only dark clumps of boughs show here and there, beneath a moonlit sky. As the curtain rises,* KATHERINE, *with brush arrested, is listening. She begins again brushing her hair, then stops, and taking a packet of letters from a drawer of her dressing-table, reads. Through the just open door behind her comes the voice of* OLIVE.

OLIVE. Mummy! I'm awake!

But KATHERINE *goes on reading; and* OLIVE *steals into the room in her nightgown.*

OLIVE. [*At* KATHERINE'S *elbow—examining her watch on its stand*] It's fourteen minutes to eleven.

KATHERINE. Olive, Olive!

OLIVE. I just wanted to see the time. I never can go to sleep if I try—it's quite helpless, you know. Is there a victory yet? [KATHERINE *shakes her head*] Oh! I prayed extra special for one in the evening papers. [*Straying round her mother*] Hasn't Daddy come?

KATHERINE. Not yet.

OLIVE. Are you waiting for him? [*Burying her face in her mother's hair*] Your hair *is* nice, Mummy. It's particular to-night.

> KATHERINE *lets fall her brush, and looks at her almost in alarm.*

OLIVE. How long has Daddy been away?

KATHERINE. Six weeks.

OLIVE. It seems about a hundred years, doesn't it? Has he been making speeches all the time?

KATHERINE. Yes.

OLIVE. To-night, too?

KATHERINE. Yes.

OLIVE. The night that man was here whose head's too bald for anything—oh! Mummy, you know—the one who cleans his teeth so termendously—I heard Daddy making a speech to the wind. It broke a wine-glass. His speeches must be good ones, mustn't they!

KATHERINE. Very.

OLIVE. It felt funny; you couldn't see any wind, you know.

KATHERINE. Talking to the wind is an expression, Olive.

OLIVE. Does Daddy often?

KATHERINE. Yes, nowadays.

OLIVE. What does it mean?

KATHERINE. Speaking to people who won't listen.

OLIVE. What do they do, then?

KATHERINE. Just a few people go to hear him, and then a great crowd comes and breaks in; or they wait for him outside, and throw things, and hoot.

OLIVE. Poor Daddy! Is it people on our side who throw things?

KATHERINE. Yes, but only rough people.

OLIVE. Why does he go on doing it? I shouldn't.

KATHERINE. He thinks it is his duty.

OLIVE. To your neighbour, or only to God?

KATHERINE. To both.

OLIVE. Oh! Are those his letters?

KATHERINE. Yes.

OLIVE. [*Reading from the letter*] "My dear Heart." Does he always call you his dear heart, Mummy? It's rather jolly, isn't it? "I shall be home about half-past ten to-morrow night. For a few hours the fires of p-u-r-g-a-t-o-r-y will cease to burn——" What are the fires of p-u-r-g-a-t-o-r-y?

KATHERINE. [*Putting away the letters*] Come, Olive!

OLIVE. But what are they?

KATHERINE. Daddy means that he's been very unhappy.

OLIVE. Have you, too?

KATHERINE. Yes.

OLIVE. [*Cheerfully*] So have I. May I open the window?

KATHERINE. No; you'll let the mist in.

OLIVE. Isn't it a funny mist—all flat!

KATHERINE. Now, come along, frog!

OLIVE. [*Making time*] Mummy, when is Uncle Hubert coming back?

KATHERINE. We don't know, dear.

OLIVE. I suppose Auntie Helen'll stay with us till he does.

KATHERINE. Yes.

OLIVE. That's something, isn't it?

KATHERINE. [*Picking her up*] Now then!

OLIVE. [*Deliciously limp*] Had I better put in the duty to your neighbour—if there isn't a victory soon? [*As they pass through the door*] You're tickling under my knee! [*Little gurgles of pleasure follow. Then silence. Then a drowsy voice*] I *must* keep awake for Daddy.

> KATHERINE *comes back. She is about to leave the door a little open, when she hears a knock on the other door. It is opened a few inches, and* NURSE'S *voice says:* "Can I come in, Ma'am?" *The* NURSE *comes in.*

KATHERINE. [*Shutting* OLIVE'S *door, and going up to her*] What is it, Nurse?

NURSE. [*Speaking in a low voice*] I've been meaning to—I'll never do it in the daytime. I'm giving you notice.

KATHERINE. Nurse! *You too!*

> *She looks towards* OLIVE's *room with dismay.*
> *The* NURSE *smudges a slow tear away from her*
> *cheek.*

NURSE. I want to go right away at once.

KATHERINE. Leave Olive! That *is* the sins of the fathers with a vengeance.

NURSE. I've had another letter from my son. No, Miss Katherine, while the master goes on upholdin' these murderin' outlandish creatures, I can't live in this house, not now he's coming back.

KATHERINE. But, Nurse——!

NURSE. It's not like them [*With an ineffable gesture*] downstairs, because I'm frightened of the mob, or of the window's bein' broke again, or mind what the boys in the street say. I should think not—no! It's my heart. I'm sore night and day thinkin' of my son, and him lying out there at night without a rag of dry clothing, and water that the bullocks won't drink, and maggots in the meat; and every day one of his friends laid out stark and cold, and one day—'imself perhaps. If anything were to 'appen to him, I'd never forgive meself—here. Ah! Miss Katherine, I wonder how you bear it—bad news comin' every day— And Sir John's face so sad— And all the time the master speaking against us, as it might be Jonah 'imself.

KATHERINE. But, Nurse, how *can* you leave us, *you?*

NURSE. [*Smudging at her cheeks*] There's that tells me it's encouragin' something to happen, if I stay here;

and Mr. More coming back to-night. You can't serve God and Mammon, the Bible says.

KATHERINE. Don't you know what it's costing him?

NURSE. Ah! Cost him his seat, and his reputation; and more than that it'll cost him, to go against the country.

KATHERINE. He's following his conscience.

NURSE. And others must follow theirs, too. No, Miss Katherine, for you to let him—you, with your three brothers out there, and your father fair wasting away with grief. Sufferin' too as you've been these three months past. What'll you feel if anything happens to my three young gentlemen out there, to my dear Mr. Hubert that I nursed myself, when your precious mother couldn't? What would she have said —with you in the camp of his enemies?

KATHERINE. Nurse, Nurse!

NURSE. In my paper they say he's encouraging these heathens and makin' the foreigners talk about us; and every day longer the war lasts, there's our blood on this house.

KATHERINE. [*Turning away*] Nurse, I can't—I won't listen.

NURSE. [*Looking at her intently*] Ah! You'll move him to leave off! I see your heart, my dear. But if you don't, then go I must!

> *She nods her head gravely, goes to the door of* OLIVE'S *room, opens it gently, stands looking for a moment, then with the words* "My Lamb!" *she goes in noiselessly and closes the door.*

KATHERINE *turns back to her glass, puts back her hair, and smooths her lips and eyes. The door from the corridor is opened, and* HELEN's *voice says:* "Kit! You're not in bed?"

KATHERINE. No.

HELEN *too is in a wrapper, with a piece of lace thrown over her head. Her face is scared and miserable, and she runs into* KATHERINE'S *arms.*

KATHERINE. My dear, what is it?

HELEN. I've seen—a vision!

KATHERINE. Hssh! You'll wake Olive!

HELEN. [*Staring before her*] I'd just fallen asleep, and I saw a plain that seemed to run into the sky— like—that fog. And on it there were—dark things. One grew into a body without a head, and a gun by its side. And one was a man sitting huddled up, nursing a wounded leg. He had the face of Hubert's servant, Wreford. And then I saw—Hubert. His face was all dark and thin; and he had—a wound, an awful wound here [*She touches her breast*]. The blood was running from it, and he kept trying to stop it— oh! Kit—by kissing it [*She pauses, stifled by emotion*]. Then I heard Wreford laugh, and say vultures didn't touch live bodies. And there came a voice, from some-where, calling out: "Oh! God! I'm dying!" And Wreford began to swear at it, and I heard Hubert say: "Don't, Wreford; let the poor fellow be!" But the voice went on and on, moaning and crying out: "I'll lie here all night dying—and then I'll die!" And

Wreford dragged himself along the ground; his face all devilish, like a man who's going to kill.

KATHERINE. My dear! How ghastly!

HELEN. Still that voice went on, and I saw Wreford take up the dead man's gun. Then Hubert got upon his feet, and went tottering along, so feebly, so dreadfully—but before he could reach and stop him, Wreford fired at the man who was crying. And Hubert called out: "You brute!" and fell right down. And when Wreford saw him lying there, he began to moan and sob, but Hubert never stirred. Then it all got black again—and I could see a dark woman-thing creeping, first to the man without a head; then to Wreford; then to Hubert, and it touched him, and sprang away. And it cried out: "A—ai—ah!" [*Pointing out at the mist*] Look! Out there! The dark things!

KATHERINE. [*Putting her arms round her*] Yes, dear, yes! You must have been looking at the mist.

HELEN. [*Strangely calm*] He's dead!

KATHERINE. It was only a dream.

HELEN. You didn't hear that cry. [*She listens*] That's Stephen. Forgive me, Kit; I oughtn't to have upset you, but I couldn't help coming.

> *She goes out.* KATHERINE, *into whom her emotion seems to have passed, turns feverishly to the window, throws it open and leans out.* MORE *comes in.*

MORE. Kit!

> *Catching sight of her figure in the window, he goes quickly to her.*

KATHERINE. Ah!   [*She has mastered her emotion.*

MORE. Let me look at you!

He draws her from the window to the candle-light, and looks long at her.

MORE. What have you done to your hair?

KATHERINE. Nothing.

MORE. It's wonderful to-night.

He takes it greedily and buries his face in it.

KATHERINE. [*Drawing her hair away*] Well?

MORE. At last!

KATHERINE. [*Pointing to* OLIVE'S *room*] Hssh!

MORE. How is she?

KATHERINE. All right.

MORE. And you?

[KATHERINE *shrugs her shoulders.*

MORE. Six weeks!

KATHERINE. Why have you come?

MORE. Why!

KATHERINE. You begin again the day after to-morrow.   Was it worth while?

MORE. Kit!

KATHERINE. It makes it harder for me, that's all.

MORE. [*Staring at her*] What's come to you?

KATHERINE. Six weeks is a long time to sit and read about your meetings.

MORE. Put that away to-night. [*He touches her*] This is what travellers feel when they come out of the desert to—water.

KATHERINE. [*Suddenly noticing the cut on his fore-head*] Your forehead!   It's cut.

MORE. It's nothing.

KATHERINE. Oh! Let me bathe it!

MORE. No, dear! It's all right.

KATHERINE. [*Turning away*] Helen has just been telling me a dream she's had of Hubert's death.

MORE. Poor child!

KATHERINE. Dream bad dreams, and wait, and hide oneself—there's been nothing else to do. Nothing, Stephen—nothing!

MORE. Hide? Because of me?

[KATHERINE *nods.*

MORE. [*With a movement of distress*] I see. I thought from your letters you were coming to feel—. Kit! You look so lovely!

Suddenly he sees that she is crying, and goes quickly to her.

MORE. My dear, don't cry! God knows I don't want to make things worse for you. I'll go away.

She draws away from him a little, and after looking long at her, he sits down at the dressing-table and begins turning over the brushes and articles of toilet, trying to find words.

MORE. Never look forward. After the time I've had—I thought—to-night—it would be summer—I thought it would be you—and everything!

While he is speaking KATHERINE *has stolen closer. She suddenly drops on her knees by his side and wraps his hand in her hair. He turns and clasps her.*

MORE. Kit!

KATHERINE. Ah! yes! But—to-morrow it begins again. Oh! Stephen! How long—how long am I to

be torn in two? [*Drawing back in his arms*] I can't—
can't bear it.

MORE. My darling!

KATHERINE. Give it up! For my sake! Give it
up! [*Pressing closer to him*] It shall be me—and everything——

MORE. God!

KATHERINE. It *shall* be—if—if——

MORE. [*Aghast*] You're not making terms? Bar-
gaining? For God's sake, Kit!

KATHERINE. For God's sake, Stephen!

MORE. You!—of all people—you!

KATHERINE. Stephen!

> *For a moment* MORE *yields utterly, then shrinks
> back.*

MORE. A bargain! It's selling my soul!

> *He struggles out of her arms, gets up, and stands
> without speaking, staring at her, and wiping
> the sweat from his forehead.* KATHERINE *re-
> mains some seconds on her knees, gazing up at
> him, not realizing. Then her head droops; she
> too gets up and stands apart, with her wrapper
> drawn close round her. It is as if a cold and
> deadly shame had come to them both. Quite
> suddenly* MORE *turns, and, without looking
> back, feebly makes his way out of the room.
> When he is gone* KATHERINE *drops on her knees
> and remains there motionless, huddled in her
> hair.*

THE CURTAIN FALLS

ACT IV

*It is between lights, the following day, in the dining-room
of* More's *house. The windows are closed, but curtains are not drawn.* Steel *is seated at the bureau,
writing a letter from* More's *dictation.*

Steel. [*Reading over the letter*] "No doubt we shall
have trouble. But, if the town authorities at the last
minute forbid the use of the hall, we'll hold the meeting
in the open. Let bills be got out, and an audience will
collect in any case."

More. They will.

Steel. "Yours truly"; I've signed for you.

[More *nods.*

Steel. [*Blotting and enveloping the letter*] You know
the servants have all given notice—except Henry.

More. Poor Henry!

Steel. It's partly nerves, of course—the windows
have been broken twice—but it's partly——

More. Patriotism. Quite! they'll do the next
smashing themselves. That reminds me—to-morrow
you begin holiday, Steel.

Steel. Oh, no!

More. My dear fellow—yes. Last night ended
your sulphur cure. Truly sorry ever to have let you
in for it.

STEEL. Some one must do the work. You're half dead as it is.

MORE. There's lots of kick in me.

STEEL. Give it up, sir. The odds are too great. It isn't worth it.

MORE. To fight to a finish; knowing you must be beaten—is anything better worth it?

STEEL. Well, then, I'm not going.

MORE. This is my private hell, Steel; you don't roast in it any longer. Believe me, it's a great comfort to hurt no one but yourself.

STEEL. I *can't* leave you, sir.

MORE. My dear boy, you're a brick—but we've got off by a miracle so far, and I can't have the responsibility of you any longer. Hand me over that correspondence about to-morrow's meeting.

> STEEL *takes some papers from his pocket, but does not hand them.*

MORE. Come! [*He stretches out his hand for the papers. As* STEEL *still draws back, he says more sharply*] Give them to me, Steel! [STEEL *hands them over*] Now, that ends it, d'you see?

> *They stand looking at each other; then* STEEL, *very much upset, turns and goes out of the room.* MORE, *who has watched him with a sorry smile, puts the papers into a dispatch-case. As he is closing the bureau, the footman* HENRY *enters, announcing:* "Mr. Mendip, sir." MENDIP *comes in, and the* FOOTMAN *withdraws.* MORE *turns to his visitor, but does not hold out his hand.*

MENDIP. [*Taking* MORE's *hand*] Give me credit for
a little philosophy, my friend. Mrs. More told me
you'd be back to-day. Have you heard?

MORE. What?

MENDIP. There's been a victory.

MORE. Thank God!

MENDIP. Ah! So you actually are flesh and blood.

MORE. Yes!

MENDIP. Take off the martyr's shirt, Stephen.
You're only flouting human nature.

MORE. So—even you defend the mob!

MENDIP. My dear fellow, you're up against the
strongest common instinct in the world. What do
you expect? That the man in the street should be a
Quixote? That his love of country should express
itself in philosophic altruism? What on earth do you
expect? Men are very simple creatures; and Mob is
just conglomerate essence of simple men.

MORE. Conglomerate *ex*crescence. Mud of street
and market-place gathered in a torrent—This blind
howling "patriotism"—what each man feels in here?
[*He touches his breast*] No!

MENDIP. You think men go beyond instinct—they
don't. All they know is that something's hurting that
image of themselves that they call country. They just
feel something big and religious, and go it blind.

MORE. This used to be the country of free speech.
It used to be the country where a man was expected
to hold to his faith.

MENDIP. There are limits to human nature, Stephen.

More. Let no man stand to his guns in face of popular attack. Still your advice, is it?

Mendip. My advice is: Get out of town at once. The torrent you speak of will be let loose the moment this news is out. Come, my dear fellow, don't stay here!

More. Thanks! I'll see that Katherine and Olive go.

Mendip. Go with them! If your cause is lost, that's no reason why *you* should be.

More. There's the comfort of not running away. And—I want comfort.

Mendip. This is bad, Stephen; bad, foolish—foolish. Well! I'm going to the House. This way?

More. Down the steps, and through the gate. Good-bye?

> Katherine *has come in followed by* Nurse, *hatted and cloaked, with a small bag in her hand.*
>
> Katherine *takes from the bureau a cheque which she hands to the* Nurse. More *comes in from the terrace.*

More. You're wise to go, Nurse.

Nurse. You've treated my poor dear badly, sir. Where's your heart?

More. In full use.

Nurse. On those heathens. Don't your own hearth and home come first? Your wife, that was born in time of war, with her own father fighting, and her grandfather killed for his country. A bitter thing,

to have the windows of her house broken, and be
pointed at by the boys in the street.

> More *stands silent under this attack, looking at
> his wife.*

KATHERINE. Nurse!

NURSE. It's unnatural, sir—what you're doing! To
think more of those savages than of your own wife!
Look at her! Did you ever see her look like that?
Take care, sir, before it's too late!

MORE. Enough, please!

> NURSE *stands for a moment doubtful; looks long at*
> KATHERINE; *then goes.*

MORE. [*Quietly*] There has been a victory.

> [*He goes out.*

> KATHERINE *is breathing fast, listening to the dis-
> tant hum and stir rising in the street. She
> runs to the window as the footman,* HENRY,
> *entering, says:* "Sir John Julian, Ma'am!"
> SIR JOHN *comes in, a newspaper in his hand.*

KATHERINE. At last! A victory!

SIR JOHN. Thank God! [*He hands her the paper.*

KATHERINE. Oh, Dad!

> *She tears the paper open, and feverishly reads.*

KATHERINE. At last!

> *The distant hum in the street is rising steadily.
> But* SIR JOHN, *after the one exultant moment
> when he handed her the paper, stares dumbly
> at the floor.*

KATHERINE. [*Suddenly conscious of his gravity*]
Father!

SIR JOHN. There is other news.

KATHERINE. One of the boys?   Hubert?

> [SIR JOHN *bows his head.*

KATHERINE. Killed?

> [SIR JOHN *again bows his head.*

KATHERINE. The dream! [*She covers her face*] Poor Helen!

> *They stand for a few seconds silent, then* SIR JOHN *raises his head, and putting up a hand, touches her wet cheek.*

SIR JOHN. [*Huskily*] Whom the gods love——

KATHERINE. Hubert!

SIR JOHN. And hulks like me go on living!

KATHERINE. Dear Dad!

SIR JOHN. But we shall drive the ruffians now!   We shall break them.   Stephen back?

KATHERINE. Last night.

SIR JOHN. Has he finished his blasphemous speech-making at last? [KATHERINE *shakes her head*] Not?

> *Then, seeing that* KATHERINE *is quivering with emotion, he strokes her hand.*

SIR JOHN. My dear!   Death is in many houses!

KATHERINE. I must go to Helen. Tell Stephen, Father. I can't.

SIR JOHN. If you wish, child.

> *She goes out, leaving* SIR JOHN *to his grave, puzzled grief; and in a few seconds* MORE *comes in.*

MORE. Yes, Sir John.   You wanted me?

SIR JOHN. Hubert is killed.

MORE. Hubert!

SIR JOHN. By these—whom you uphold. Katherine asked me to let you know. She's gone to Helen. I understand you only came back last night from your—— No word I can use would give what I feel about that. I don't know how things stand now between you and Katherine; but I tell you this, Stephen: you've tried her these last two months beyond what any woman ought to bear!

[MORE *makes a gesture of pain*

SIR JOHN. When you chose your course——

MORE. Chose!

SIR JOHN. You placed yourself in opposition to every feeling in her. You knew this might come. It may come again with another of my sons——

MORE. I would willingly change places with any one of them.

SIR JOHN. Yes—I can believe in your unhappiness. I cannot conceive of greater misery than to be arrayed against your country. If I could have Hubert back, I would not have him at such a price—no, nor all my sons. *Pro patriâ mori*—— My boy, at all events, is happy!

MORE. Yes!

SIR JOHN. Yet you can go on doing what you are! What devil of pride has got into you, Stephen?

MORE. Do you imagine I think myself better than the humblest private fighting out there? Not for a minute.

SIR JOHN. I don't understand you. I always thought you devoted to Katherine.

MORE. Sir John, you believe that country comes before wife and child?

SIR JOHN. I do.

MORE. So do I.

SIR JOHN. [*Bewildered*] Whatever my country does or leaves undone, I no more presume to judge her than I presume to judge my God. [*With all the exaltation of the suffering he has undergone for her*] My country!

MORE. I would give all I have—for that creed.

SIR JOHN. [*Puzzled*] Stephen, I've never looked on you as a crank; I always believed you sane and honest. But this is—visionary mania.

MORE. Vision of what might be.

SIR JOHN. Why can't you be content with what the grandest nation—the grandest men on earth—have found good enough for them? I've known them, I've seen what they could suffer, for our country.

MORE. Sir John, imagine what the last two months have been to me! To see people turn away in the street—old friends pass me as if I were a wall! To dread the post! To go to bed every night with the sound of hooting in my ears! To know that my name is never referred to without contempt——

SIR JOHN. You have your new friends. Plenty of them, I understand.

MORE. Does that make up for being spat at as I was last night? Your battles are fool's play to it.

The stir and rustle of the crowd in the street grows louder. SIR JOHN *turns his head towards it.*

SIR JOHN. You've heard there's been a victory. Do

you carry your unnatural feeling so far as to be sorry for that? [MORE *shakes his head*] That's something! For God's sake, Stephen, stop before it's gone past mending. Don't ruin your life with Katherine. Hubert was her favourite brother; you are backing those who killed him. Think what that means to her! Drop this—mad Quixotism—idealism—whatever you call it. Take Katherine away. Leave the country till the thing's over—this country of yours that you're opposing, and—and—traducing. Take her away! Come! What good are you doing? What earthly good? Come, my boy! Before you're utterly undone.

MORE. Sir John! Our men are dying out there for the faith that's in them! I believe my faith the higher, the better for mankind—— Am I to slink away? Since I began this campaign I've found hundreds who've thanked me for taking this stand. They look on me now as their leader. Am I to desert them? When you led your forlorn hope—did you ask yourself what good you were doing, or whether you'd come through alive? It's my forlorn hope not to betray those who are following me; and not to help let die a fire—a fire that's sacred—not only now in this country, but in all countries, for all time.

SIR JOHN. [*After a long stare*] I give you credit for believing what you say. But let me tell you whatever that fire you talk of—I'm too old-fashioned to grasp—one fire you *are* letting die—your wife's love. By God! This crew of your new friends, this crew of cranks and jays, if they can make up to you for the loss of her love—of your career, of all those who used to like and respect you—so much the better for you. But if you find yourself bankrupt of affection—alone as the last man on earth; if this business ends in your utter ruin and destruction—as it must—I shall not pity—I cannot pity you. Good-night!

> *He marches to the door, opens it, and goes out.*
> MORE *is left standing perfectly still. The stir and murmur of the street is growing all the time, and slowly forces itself on his consciousness. He goes to the bay window and looks out; then rings the bell. It is not answered, and, after turning up the lights, he rings again.* KATHERINE *comes in. She is wearing a black hat, and black outdoor coat. She speaks coldly without looking up.*

KATHERINE. You rang!

MORE. For them to shut this room up.

KATHERINE. The servants have gone out. They're afraid of the house being set on fire.

MORE. I see.

KATHERINE. They have not your ideals to sustain them. [MORE *winces*] I am going with Helen and Olive to Father's.

MORE. [*Trying to take in the exact sense of her words*] Good! You prefer that to an hotel? [KATHERINE *nods. Gently*] Will you let me say, Kit, how terribly I feel for you—Hubert's——

KATHERINE. Don't. I ought to have made what I meant plainer. I am not coming back.

MORE. Not——? Not while the house——

KATHERINE. Not—at all.

MORE. Kit!

KATHERINE. I warned you from the first. You've gone too far!

MORE. [*Terribly moved*] Do you understand what this means? After ten years—and all—our love!

KATHERINE. *Was* it love? How could you ever have loved one so unheroic as myself!

MORE. This is madness, Kit—Kit!

KATHERINE. Last night I was ready. You couldn't. If you couldn't then, you never can. You are very exalted, Stephen. I don't like living—I won't live, with one whose equal I am not. This has been coming ever since you made that speech. I told you that night what the end would be.

MORE. [*Trying to put his arms round her*] Don't be so terribly cruel!

KATHERINE. No! Let's have the truth! People so wide apart don't love! Let me go!

MORE. In God's name, how can I help the difference in our faiths?

KATHERINE. Last night you used the word—bargain. Quite right. I meant to buy you. I meant to kill your faith. You showed me what I was doing. I don't like to be shown up as a driver of bargains, Stephen.

MORE. God knows—I never meant——

KATHERINE. If I'm not yours in spirit—I don't choose to be your—mistress.

MORE, *as if lashed by a whip, has thrown up his hands in an attitude of defence.*

KATHERINE. Yes, that's cruel! It shows the heights you live on. I won't drag you down.

MORE. For God's sake, put your pride away, and *see!* I'm fighting for the faith that's in me. What else can a man do? What else? Ah! Kit! Do see!

KATHERINE. I'm strangled here! Doing nothing—sitting silent—when my brothers are fighting, and being killed. I shall try to go out nursing. Helen will come with me. I have my faith, too; my poor common love of country. I can't stay here with you. I spent last night on the floor—thinking—and I know!

MORE. And Olive?

KATHERINE. I shall leave her at Father's, with Nurse; unless you forbid me to take her. You can.

MORE. [*Icily*] That I shall not do—you know very well. You are free to go, and to take her.

KATHERINE. [*Very low*] Thank you! [*Suddenly she turns to him, and draws his eyes on her. Without a sound, she puts her whole strength into that look*] Stephen! Give it up! Come down to me!

> *The festive sounds from the street grow louder. There can be heard the blowing of whistles, and bladders, and all the sounds of joy.*

MORE. And drown in—*that?*

> KATHERINE *turns swiftly to the door. There she stands and again looks at him. Her face is mysterious, from the conflicting currents of her emotions.*

MORE. So—you're going?

KATHERINE. [*In a whisper*] Yes.

> *She bends her head, opens the door, and goes.*
> MORE *starts forward as if to follow her, but*
> OLIVE *has appeared in the doorway. She has*
> *on a straight little white coat and a round white*
> *cap.*

OLIVE. Aren't you coming with us, Daddy?

> [MORE *shakes his head.*

OLIVE. Why not?

MORE. Never mind, my dicky bird.

OLIVE. The motor'll have to go very slow. There
are such a lot of people in the street. Are you staying
to stop them setting the house on fire? [MORE *nods*]
May I stay a little, too? [MORE *shakes his head*] Why?

MORE. [*Putting his hand on her head*] Go along, my
pretty!

OLIVE. Oh! love me up, Daddy!

> [MORE *takes and loves her up*

OLIVE. Oo-o!

MORE. Trot, my soul!

> *She goes, looks back at him, turns suddenly, and*
> *vanishes.*
> MORE *follows her to the door, but stops there.*
> *Then, as full realization begins to dawn on him,*
> *he runs to the bay window, craning his head to*
> *catch sight of the front door. There is the sound*
> *of a vehicle starting, and the continual hooting*
> *of its horn as it makes its way among the crowd*
> *He turns from the window.*

MORE. Alone as the last man on earth!

    Suddenly a voice rises clear out of the hurly-burly in the street.

VOICE. There 'e is! That's 'im! More! Traitor! More!

    A shower of nutshells, orange-peel, and harmless missiles begins to rattle against the glass of the window. Many voices take up the groaning: "More! Traitor! Black-leg! More!" And through the window can be seen waving flags and lighted Chinese lanterns, swinging high on long bamboos. The din of execration swells. MORE stands unheeding, still gazing after the cab. Then, with a sharp crack, a flung stone crashes through one of the panes. It is followed by a hoarse shout of laughter, and a hearty groan. A second stone crashes through the glass. MORE turns for a moment, with a contemptuous look, towards the street, and the flare of the Chinese lanterns lights up his face. Then, as if forgetting all about the din outside, he moves back into the room, looks round him, and lets his head droop. The din rises louder and louder; a third stone crashes through. MORE raises his head again, and, clasping his hands, looks straight before him. The footman, HENRY, entering, hastens to the French windows.

MORE. Ah! Henry, I thought you'd gone.

FOOTMAN. I came back, sir.

MORE. Good fellow!

FOOTMAN. They're trying to force the terrace gate, sir. They've no business coming on to private property—no matter what!

> *In the surging entrance of the mob the footman,* HENRY, *who shows fight, is overwhelmed, hustled out into the crowd on the terrace, and no more seen.* The MOB *is a mixed crowd of revellers of both sexes, medical students, clerks, shop men and girls, and a Boy Scout or two. Many have exchanged hats—some wear masks, or false noses, some carry feathers or tin whistles. Some, with bamboos and Chinese lanterns, swing them up outside on the terrace. The medley of noises is very great. Such ringleaders as exist in the confusion are a* GROUP OF STUDENTS, *the chief of whom, conspicuous because unadorned, is an athletic, hatless young man with a projecting underjaw, and heavy coal-black moustache, who seems with the swing of his huge arms and shoulders to sway the currents of motion. When the first surge of noise and movement subsides, he calls out:* "To him, boys! Chair the hero!" THE STUDENTS *rush at the impassive* MORE, *swing him roughly on to their shoulders and bear him round the room. When they have twice circled the table to the music of their confused singing, groans and whistling,* THE CHIEF OF THE STUDENTS *calls out:* "Put him down!" *Obediently they set him down on the table which has been forced*

into the bay window, and stand gaping up at him.

CHIEF STUDENT. Speech!   Speech!

The noise ebbs, and MORE *looks round him.*

CHIEF STUDENT. Now then, you, sir.

MORE. [*In a quiet voice*] Very well.   You are here by the law that governs the action of all mobs—the law of Force.   By that law, you can do what you like to this body of mine.

A VOICE. And we will, too.

MORE. I don't doubt it.   But before that, I've a word to say.

A VOICE. You've always that.

[ANOTHER VOICE *raises a donkey's braying.*]

MORE. You—Mob—are the most contemptible thing under the sun.   When you walk the street—God goes in.

CHIEF STUDENT. Be careful, you—sir.

VOICES. Down him!   Down with the beggar!

MORE. [*Above the murmurs*] My fine friends, I'm not afraid of you.   You've forced your way into my house, and you've asked me to speak.   Put up with the truth for once! [*His words rush out*] You are the thing that pelts the weak; kicks women; howls down free speech.   This to-day, and that to-morrow.   Brain —you have none.   Spirit—not the ghost of it!   If you're not meanness, there's no such thing.   If you're not cowardice, there is no cowardice [*Above the grow- ing fierceness of the hubbub*] Patriotism—there are two

kinds—that of our soldiers, and this of mine. You
have neither!

CHIEF STUDENT. [*Checking a dangerous rush*] Hold
on! Hold on! [*To* MORE] Swear to utter no more
blasphemy against your country: Swear it!

CROWD. Ah! Ay! Ah!

MORE. My country is not yours. Mine is that great
country which shall never take toll from the weakness
of others. [*Above the groaning*] Ah! you can break my
head and my windows; but don't think that you can
break my faith. You could never break or shake it,
if you were a million to one.

> *A girl with dark eyes and hair all wild, leaps out
> from the crowd and shakes her fist at him.*

GIRL. You're friends with them that killed my lad!
[MORE *smiles down at her, and she swiftly plucks the
knife from the belt of a Boy Scout beside her*] Smile,
you—cur!

> *A violent rush and heave from behind flings* MORE
> *forward on to the steel. He reels, staggers back,
> and falls down amongst the crowd. A scream,
> a sway, a rush, a hubbub of cries. The* CHIEF
> STUDENT *shouts above the riot:* "Steady!"
> *Another:* "My God! He's got it!"

CHIEF STUDENT. Give him air!

> *The crowd falls back, and two* STUDENTS, *bending
> over* MORE, *lift his arms and head, but they fall
> like lead. Desperately they test him for life.*

CHIEF STUDENT. By the Lord, it's over!

> *Then begins a scared swaying out towards the*

*window.   Some one turns out the lights, and in
the darkness the crowd fast melts away.   The
body of* MORE *lies in the gleam from a single
Chinese lantern.   Muttering the words:* "Poor
devil! He kept his end up anyway!" *the*
CHIEF STUDENT *picks from the floor a little
abandoned Union Jack and lays it on* MORE'S
breast.   Then he, too, turns, and rushes out.
And the body of MORE *lies in the streak of light;
and the noises in the street continue to rise.*

THE CURTAIN FALLS, BUT RISES AGAIN ALMOST
AT ONCE.

AFTERMATH

A late Spring dawn is just breaking. Against trees in leaf and blossom, with the houses of a London Square beyond, suffused by the spreading glow, is seen a dark life-size statue on a granite pedestal. In front is the broad, dust-dim pavement. The light grows till the central words around the pedestal can be clearly read:

ERECTED

To the Memory

of

STEPHEN MORE

"Faithful to his ideal"

High above, the face of MORE *looks straight before him with a faint smile. On one shoulder and on his bare head two sparrows have perched, and from the gardens, behind, comes the twittering and singing of birds.*

THE CURTAIN FALLS.

END

14

Date Due